Facing ICT Challenges in the Era of Social

Zoran Levnajić (ed.)

Facing ICT Challenges
in the Era of Social Media

Bibliographic Information published by the Deutsche Nationalbibliothek
The Deutsche Nationalbibliothek lists this publication in the Deutsche Nationalbibliografie; detailed bibliographic data is available in the internet at http://dnb.d-nb.de.

Library of Congress Cataloging-in-Publication Data
Facing ICT challenges in the era of social media / Levnajic, Zoran (ed.).
    pages cm
    ISBN 978-3-631-65383-8 — ISBN 978-3-653-04602-1 (ebook)
    1. Information technology. I. Levnajic, Zoran, 1977–
    T58.5.F259 2014
    303.48'33—dc23
                                                    2014017239

ISBN 978-3-631-65383-8 (Print)
E-ISBN 978-3-653-04602-1 (E-Book)
DOI 10.3726/978-3-653-04602-1

© Peter Lang GmbH
Internationaler Verlag der Wissenschaften
Frankfurt am Main 2014
All rights reserved.
PL Academic Research is an Imprint of Peter Lang GmbH.

Peter Lang – Frankfurt am Main · Bern · Bruxelles · New York ·
Oxford · Warszawa · Wien

www.peterlang.com

Acknowledgements

This publication is funded by the Creative Core FISNM-3330–13-500033 'Simulations' project funded by the European Union, The European Regional Development Fund. The operation is carried out within the framework of the Operational Programme for Strengthening Regional Development Potentials for the period 2007–2013, Development Priority 1: Competitiveness and research excellence, Priority Guideline 1.1: Improving the competitive skills and research excellence.

**Fakulteta za
informacijske študije**
Faculty of information studies

REPUBLIKA SLOVENIJA
**MINISTRSTVO ZA IZOBRAŽEVANJE,
ZNANOST IN ŠPORT**

Naložba v vašo prihodnost
OPERACIJO DELNO FINANCIRA EVROPSKA UNIJA
Evropski socialni sklad

Kreativno jedro:
Simulacije
Creative core: Simulations

»Operacijo delno financira Evropska unija, in sicer iz Evropskega sklada za regionalni razvoj. Operacija se izvaja v okviru Operativnega program krepitve regionalnih razvojnih potencialov za obdobje 2007-2013, 1. razvojne prioritete: Konkurenčnost podjetij in raziskovalna odličnost, prednostne usmeritve 1.1: Izboljšanje konkurenčnih sposobnosti podjetij in raziskovalna odličnost.

Table of Contents

Preface

World Wide Web is becoming a utility, not unlike electricity or running water in our homes. This creates new ways of using the web, where Social media plays a particular role. This gives an unprecedented opportunity to study the emerging social phenomena in the virtual world. In addition, it opens new avenues for improving public services such as schooling. This book includes some of the latest developments in employing the information and communications technologies for examining both virtual and real-life social interactions. Investigating modern challenges such as online education, web security or organized cybercrime, this book outlines the state of the art in social applications and implications of ICT.

Issues of Collaboration in a Virtual Environment

Blaž Rodič

Faculty of Information Studies in Novo mesto, Slovenia

Abstract

With the globalization of the economy, more and more employees are working with team members half way around the world. This paper examines the benefits and issues in using information technologies, including Web 2.0, to support collaboration of teams in a virtual environment, the emerging methods and technologies and socio-technical issues associated with collaboration and teams in virtual environments, and proposes a new categorization of e-collaboration tools, which supplements the older classifications. In order to reduce the negative effects, developers and users of e-collaboration tools for virtual environments should address human interaction issues as well as social issues and organizational issues.

Keywords

e-collaboration, virtual teams, virtual environment, HCI, globalization

1. Introduction

Advancing research in the area of human-computer interaction, smart environments, multi-modal interaction, ambient intelligence and ubiquitous computing nowadays is converging into the dawning era of human computing (Pantic et al., 2006). Human computing escalates the complexities of human-human and human-machine interaction in the already complex software engineering and system integration (Clancey, 1997). Emerging e-collaboration systems are expected to be increasingly adapted to the nature of human cognition and communication and present a quantum leap beyond modern productivity-oriented workplace technologies in which performance is the key objective and the user experience comes after business process logic and formalized workflow.

To understand the current limitations, i.e. opportunities for improvement in e-collaboration tools and concepts and possible issues, we first need to define e-collaboration itself. Kock (2005) stated that e-collaboration consists of the following elements:

- The collaborative task: A task that parties can work on together. For example, jobs beyond the capacity of one organization, or jobs that require complementary skill sets;
- The e-collaboration technology: Existing or new IT infrastructure such as teleconferencing, discussion boards and instant messaging;
- The participants: Organizations that are collaborating, industry associations and government agencies. Characteristics of the participants and size of the group can also have an effect on the collaboration.
- Mental schemas of the participants: The knowledge and experience of the participants and the degree of similarity between participants. For example, expert or novice understanding of the task.
- The physical environment: The location of the participants. For example, the geographical location of the toolmakers was dispersed and therefore they needed to apply more effort to e-collaboration, whereas the IT organizations were within the same geographical area;
- The social environment: the perceptions of trust and the behaviour among the participants as well as peer pressure among participants.

An ever-increasing number of e-collaboration systems and solutions have been developed recently. E-collaboration can be categorized according to the time and space where/when the participants are present. The space dimension is discrete, while the dimension of artificiality (nature of a participant's presentation in the software) can use several different combinations of realistic and synthetic representations. We have combined the model of shared spaces proposed by Benford et al. (1998), which focuses on synchronous communication with the categorization of several types of groupware tools. Our proposed categorization of groupware is shown in Table 1. This new categorization gives a better insight into the relation between the dimensions of artificiality, space, time, and the type of tools available. Several examples of tools are listed in multiple categories, as their flexibility allows usage under synchronous and asynchronous conditions and the choice of representation is left to the user. It is also evident that some modes of collaboration are supported by more tools than other modes. E.g. tools made specifically for asynchronous collaboration at the same location are rare, as location is generally not relevant for asynchronous collaboration.

Table 1: *Proposed categorization of e-collaboration systems according to time, space and artificiality*

<table>
<tr><td rowspan="9">DIMENSION OF ARTIFICIALITY</td><td rowspan="4">Synthetic (generated)</td><td>Augmented Reality</td><td>Virtual Reality</td></tr>
<tr><td>Same time
(synchronous)</td><td>Same time
(synchronous)
e.g. virtual worlds, chat</td></tr>
<tr><td>Different time (asynchronous)</td><td>Different time (asynchronous)
e.g. virtual worlds, forums, wikis</td></tr>
<tr><td>Physical Reality</td><td>Tele-Presence</td></tr>
<tr><td rowspan="4">Physical (real/istic)</td><td>Same time
(synchronous)
e.g. e-meetings, e-voting, e-brain-storming</td><td>Same time
(synchronous)
e.g. teleconferencing, e-meetings, screen sharing, shared documents, chat</td></tr>
<tr><td rowspan="2">Different time (asynchronous)
e.g. collaborative design</td><td>Different time (asynchronous)
e.g. workflow tools, document management systems, email, shared documents, forums</td></tr>
<tr><td colspan="2" style="text-align:center">Local (physically present)   Remote (represented)
Dimension Of Space</td></tr>
</table>

For example, electronic meeting tools can provide participants that are present at the same time, either at the same or different locations with the following benefits:

- Interactive systems supporting synchronous, non-structured decision processes.
- Provide methodological support in analysis of a problem and drafting of solutions (Systematic and documented discussion).
- Provide tools for automation of several aspects of the meeting, e.g.:
  – Keeping meeting minutes,
  – Brainstorming (empty sheet concept),
  – Group categorization, ranking, voting,
- Parallel and shared activities instead of turn-by-turn (submission of ideas, categorization) and anonymity of participants, which can drastically improve the efficiency of meetings.

2. E-collaboration Tool Development Trends

A new type of e-collaboration has recently emerged that is not product of the thousands of man-years and millions of dollars, invested in the development of formal eCollaboration solutions (usually proprietary and created by professionals): the dark horse is user-created and community-driven e-collaboration, produced by volunteers, and freely available. In the world of new collaborative media, content is increasingly created by users, enhanced by community contribution, and accessed through open platforms, particularly Web 2.0 based platforms.

Web 2.0 platforms are technologies, which enable users to form up virtual communities in order to interact and communicate over the Internet. A virtual community can be defined as a group of people sharing common interests by using Internet applications. Nowadays an increasing number of companies and non-governmental and non-profit organizations set up virtual communities (McAfee, 2006; O'Reilly, 2005). Virtual communities implemented by companies promise to improve the knowledge management by integrating customers in the value creation chain. As a means of customer relationship management, virtual communities contribute to increase the customer loyalty and a deeper understanding of customer needs (Lattemann & Stieglitz, 2007). Web 2.0 driven social software comprises a couple of innovative technological approaches, which in particular are key elements of virtual community infrastructures. Virtual communities allow members to share knowledge, experiences, opinions, and ideas with each other.

The term Web 2.0 was coined around the year 2005 and describes new interactive applications on the internet (O'Reilly, 2005). However most technological improvements comprised by the term web 2.0 have already been invented years before ((O'Reilly, 2005) and (McAfee, 2006)). Web 2.0 applications are often associated with "social software". Whereas traditional software focuses on productivity and process support, web 2.0 applications focus on enabling communication, cooperation, and collaboration of individuals and groups over the internet. Social software is based on different services for setting up networks and supporting the distribution of information within the network (e.g. e-mail, instant messaging, chats, or blogs) (Stieglitz et al., 2008).

However, social e-collaboration systems can become a compliance and control nightmare and introduce the risk of information leaks and public relations problems. Most companies therefore aim to either regulate or ban non-company e-collaboration systems. However if the CEOs of yesteryear wondered whether to ban Facebook and other social networks during work hours outright, today's CEOs wonder how to make employees use them effectively for their business needs.

One way of making Web 2.0 more acceptable to executives and security managers is the use of the platform in the development of proprietary, company controlled e-collaboration systems. This approach has brought the advent of Enterprise 2.0. While Web 2.0 is originally about the development and usage of new ways of communication and tools for this in the public; Enterprise 2.0 is about organizationally focused support of collaboration in the enterprise. Enterprise 2.0 aims to help employees, customers and suppliers collaborate, share, and organize information via Web 2.0 technologies. McAfee (2006) describes Enterprise 2.0 as "the use of emergent social software platforms within companies, or between companies and their partners or customers"

To be honest, most concepts in what is now is advertised as a revolution on the Web or Enterprise 2.0 have been used in companies as CSCW (Computer-Supported Collaborative Work) applications since the 1970s. However, the tools of old were not nearly as intuitive, adaptable and usable as today, and the technologies that have been developed since then allow us to make e-collaboration tools accessible beyond the walls of companies.

Virtual environments and mobile technologies bring business scenarios closer to the 24/7, anytime, anywhere vision (Kalakota & Robinson, 2001). Virtual communities are set up by companies in order to bridge the gap between customers and companies and thus serve as a customer relationship management tool (Stieglitz et al., 2008). A good example are collaborative Customer Relations Management (CRM) technologies, which allow collaboration and instant sharing of relevant information among employees at different locations, which can improve customer service and increase customer involvement in the business processes (e.g. product design, creation, sales and marketing). The results (Reinhold & Alt, 2009) can be a higher alignment of business offerings with customer needs, optimization of internal business processes with customer feedback and an increased customer satisfaction with the delivered services.

One interesting model developed in CSCW or e-collaboration systems for understanding different modes of communication in groups is the people/artifact framework which tackles the functional relationship between members and the tools to support collaboration, and maps out these relationships in a way that allows designers to follow the flow of information within the system (Dix et al., 1993). Figure 1 shows the principle of this framework. The directional and bi-directional connections indicate channels of communication either between participants or between a participant and the artefact.

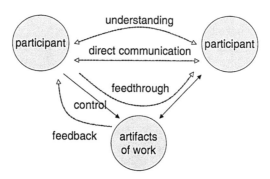

Fig. 1: People/artifact framework model (Dix et al 1993)

Main goal of eCollaboration systems is to reduce the isolation of users from each other (Koch & Gross, 2006). eCollaboration systems explicitly provide awareness of the users and their activities. Lynch et al. pointed out in 1990 that eCollaboration systems are distinguished from normal software by making the user aware that they is part of a group, while most other software seeks to hide and protect users from each other (Lynch et al., 1990). eCollaboration systems can include software, hardware, services or group process support. The classification according to the main mode of interaction as proposed by (Sauter et al., 1994) is presented in Figure 2.

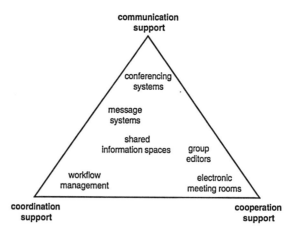

Fig. 2: Classification of eCollaboration systems by the main mode of interaction supported (Sauter et al., 1994)

3. Human Interaction Issues

Even if the development of technologies and concepts in e-collaboration tools has been impressive, there are still aspects of human collaboration and inter-action that are yet not sufficiently supported. While "ICT allows organizations to bridge time and distance barriers with once undreamed of ease" (Kasper-Fuehrer & Ashkanasy, 2001), it also creates new boundaries at the level of the work unit (Breu & Hemingway, 2004). Scholars have shown that computer-mediated communication can lead to severe problems of interpreting transmit-ted information (Andres, 2002).

Most of the nonverbal cues that we take for granted in face-to-face com-munication are not transferred in online communications: these include spatial orientation, body posture, hand gesture, glancing, and facial expression. Fur-thermore, users typically have a very limited awareness of others, who may silently "lurk" in text-based environments (Preece, 2000).

Teleconferencing does not provide body language or other spatial cues – gaze direction, spatial presence and direct or peripheral awareness of the activ-ity of participants. Videoconferencing does not create a feeling of co-location: you can't place people in relation to one another; other than knowing that someone is looking at the camera; you cannot tell what they are looking at (Benford et al., 1997).

Facial expressions are the basic way of expressing emotion, agreement or disagreement and understanding or confusion. Glancing and eye contact are another important aspects of body language. As with body orientation, the direction of a person's gaze indicates their focus of attention: it is used for ini-tiating, maintaining, and ending a conversation. It is also used extensively in group conversations, which require non-verbal turn-taking cues. To overcome these limitations of telecommunication, emotional icons are used extensively in text-based environments including emails, chats, forums and instant mes-saging to give users the ability to express emotion. Real-life communication however makes far more extensive use of non-verbal mechanisms. The social subtleties of gaze and eye contact require a strong degree of presence within a virtual environment for them to work effectively. (Redfern & Naughton, 2002)

Real-time modeled human-like representations (avatars) give the poten-tial for body language to be included as a communication channel. While the graphics of most virtual environments have generally been rather unso-phisticated, studies have shown that even crude block-like forms of avatars can be useful in communicating non-verbal social cues (Tromp & Snowdon,

1997). Despite the graphic simplicity, a user's awareness of the spatial proximity and orientation of others has a strong impact on the dynamics of group communication.

A greater level of realism and support for non-verbal communication can be developed within collaborative virtual environments (CVEs), which are computer-enabled, distributed virtual spaces or places in which people can meet and interact with others, with agents and with virtual objects. CVEs vary greatly in their representational richness from 3D virtual reality to 2D and even text based environments. The main applications to date have been military and industrial team training, collaborative design and engineering, and multiplayer games.

CVEs clearly have the potential to enable innovative and effective distance teaching techniques, involving for example debate, simulation, role play, discussion groups, brainstorming, and project-based group work. The emphasis can be placed on the human-to-human interactions as common understandings are negotiated and developed across differences of knowledge, skills and attitudes.

4. Social Issues

Apart from the human interaction, another area that needs to be further developed in e-collaboration systems is their support for existing socio-technical systems and their improvement. For an online environment to be successful, there have to be good reasons for people to use it. For work-driven e-collaboration, this is known to include the provision of useful collaborative tools within the environment. However for social e-collaboration, this should also include mechanisms for fostering social activity – something that has rarely been recognized in CVE research (Redfern & Naughton, 2002). E.g. chance meetings; informal and unplanned meetings with colleagues are rarely supported in e-collaboration tools, yet they are known to be crucial to the work of many workers, particularly knowledge workers. Informal meetings are crucial to the work activities (development of a team spirit) and for a meeting to take place, a synchronous, rather than asynchronous awareness is indispensable. A meeting space does not come into being unless synchronous awareness is realized.

The technical system and the social system have to be co-optimized for the whole system to be successful. If a technical system is created or introduced at the expense of a social system, the obtained results will be sub-optimal. The main messages from the socio-technical systems discussion for e-collaboration are (Koch, 2008):

• technical systems (e-collaboration support technology) are highly embedded in social systems,
• the social and the technical subsystems should be optimized (designed) in parallel, because they influence each other,
• the goal/task of the overall system should not be forgotten – it usually is a main source for the coherence of the system.

In this context it is important to note that implementing an eCollaboration system should mean designing a complete socio-technical system, including organizational and social aspects. The technical aspect is less important that the socio-technical aspect. As many collaboration aspects are common to different eCollaboration and Web 2.0 systems, they are implemented in (sometimes freely) available components, which can be reused. Therefore it is common that a new eCollaboration is not developed from scratch and off-the-shelf components are used instead. Development therefore means selection, adaptation, integration and configuration.

5. Management Issues

Several management and organization challenges are also associated with virtualizing organization structures. Through virtualization the complexity of the organization can increase drastically, because of new barriers and inter-group interfaces (Andres, 2002). Especially challenging is the management of a multi-project (e.g. matrix) organization where most employees work on several project concurrently. At the group level, new problems of information exchange and knowledge sharing arise due to the emergence of new spatial and social barriers in distributed environments (Andres, 2002). In distributed work arrangements people are often left out of important decision processes (remoteness), which can cause unnecessary conflicts at the team level (Grinter et al., 1999).

Moreover, in the virtualized organization people have to show social competencies and to learn to act as boundary spanners to ensure knowledge sharing (Breu & Hemingway, 2004). From a human resource perspective further problems are posed by the control and incentive aspects of the new work settings (Riemer & Vehring, 2008): controlling people and their work processes becomes much more challenging once traditional co-located settings are given up.

6. Conclusion

To summarize, in order to successfully implement e-collaboration systems also from the social aspect, the company culture often has to adapt to the new collaboration possibilities brought by the e-collaboration system. We can come close to the ideal by involving the employees as much as possible in the design of the e-collaboration system – to do a participatory design of the work systems (the whole socio-technical system including technology but also organizational and social aspects. For example in an implementation of an intranet social network system, the team leader should involve all team members from the beginning. Ideally, one would start with a discussion to identify the business processes to be supported with the social network.

The need to include "some bottom-up" initiative in the introduction of eCollaboration systems can also be explained by the status of eCollaboration systems in the typical IT organization. eCollaboration systems lies in between individual productivity software – where individual value and motivation is of core importance – and large systems where strong backing by upper management is critical to success.

The companies' experience with Facebook and similar social sites shows that the user motivation to use social software is higher than using classical eCollaboration systems, and the main difference may be the possibility to "have fun". Social software is built for being a 'medium', i.e. being flexible to be used in different settings for different – not yet envisioned – tasks, while eCollaboration tools are relatively rigid, focused on the work tasks and leave users too little freedom. Since every cooperation scenario is different, and even in one setup the needs are constantly changing, users of rigid platforms have to work around the platform more and more, while users of media-like platforms just use the medium in new ways.

To ensure that the coworkers still collaborate efficiently if provided with an open collaboration media a company should not restrict the possibilities, but rather by help the users to explore the possibilities and to avoid errors others have made before. Key to success is to strike the right balance between providing the right guidelines and leaving enough freedom for users to develop their own ways of using the e-collaboration tools, and monitor the evolving process in order to identify problems and good practices. Insufficient guidance might lead to an ineffective diversity, but too much guidance might kill the important "fun factor". Consequently, the guidelines should be developed in a participative approach in close cooperation with the end users.

Bibliography

Andres, H. P., A comparison of face-to-face and virtual software development teams, Team Performance Management, Vol. 8, No. 1/2, pp. 39–48, 2002.

Benford, S., Greenhalgh, C., Reynard, G., Briwn, C., and Koleva, B., Understanding and constructing shared spaces with mixed reality boundaries. ACM Transactions on Computer-Human Interaction (ToCHI), 5(3), pp. 185–223, 1998.

Benford, S., Snowdon, D., Colebourne, A., O'Brien, J. & Rodden, T., Informing the Design of Collaborative Virtual Environments. Proceedings ACM GROUP '97, pp. 71–80, 1997.

Breu, K. & Hemingway, C. J., Making organisations virtual: the hidden cost of distributed teams, Journal of Information Technology, Vol. 19, No. 3, pp. 191–202, 2004.

Clancey, W., Situated Cognition: On Human Knowledge and Computer Representations. Cambridge: Cambridge University Press, 1997.

Dix, A. J., Finley, J., Abowd, G. D. & Beale, R., Human-Computer Interaction. New York, Prentice Hall, 1993.

Grinter, R. E., Herbsleb, J. D. & Perry, D. E., The Geography of Coordination: Dealing with Distance in R&D Work, in "Proceedings of the Proceedings of the International ACM SIGGROUP Conference on Supporting Group Work (GROUP '99)", New York, ACM Press, pp. 306–315, 1999.

Kalakota, R., & Robinson, M. (2001). M-Business: The race to mobility, New York, McGraw-Hill Companies.

Kasper-Fuehrer, E. C. & Ashkanasy, N. M., Communicating trustworthiness and building trust in interorganizational virtual organizations, Journal of Management Information Systems, Vol. 27, pp. 235–254, 2001.

Koch, M. & Gross, T. (2006). Computer-Supported Cooperative Work – Concepts and Trends. In:Proc. Conf. of the Association Information And Management (AIM), Lecture Notes in Informatics (LNI) P-92, Bonn, Koellen Verlag.

Koch, M., CSCW and Enterprise 2.0 – towards an Integrated Perspective, 21st Bled eConference Collaboration:Overcoming Boundaries Through Multi-Channel Interaction, June 15–18, 2008; Bled, Slovenia, 2008.

Kock, N., What is e-collaboration?, International Journal of e- Collaboration, Vol. 1, No. 1, pp. i–vii, 2005.

Lattemann, C. & Stieglitz, S. (2007). Online Communities for Customer Relationship Management on Financial Stock Markets – A Case Study from a Project at the Berlin Stock Exchange. In: Proceedings of the "Americas Conference on Information Systems (AMCIS)", August 2007.

Lynch, K. J., Snyder, J. M., Vogel, D. M. & McHenry, W. K. (1990). The Arizona Analyst Information System: Supporting Collaborative Research on International Technological Trends. In: Gibbs, S.; Verrijn-Stuart, A. A.: Multi-User Interfaces and Applications, Amsterdam, Elsevier Science, pp. 159–174.

McAfee, A., Enterprise 2.0: The Dawn of Emergent Collaboration, MIT Sloan Management Review, No. 47, Vol. 3, pp. 21–28, 2006.

O'Reilly, T., What is Web 2.0: Design Patterns and Business Models for the Next Generation of Software. Koln, O'Reilly-Verlag, 2005.

Pantic, M., Pentland, A., Nijholt, A., & Huang, T., Human computing and machine understanding of human behavior: A survey. In Kwek, F. and Yang, Y., editors, ACM SIGCHI Proceedings Eighth International Conference on Multimodal Interfaces (ACM ICMI 2006), pages 239–248, Banff, Canada. ACM, New York, 2006.

Preece, J., Online Communities: Designing Usability, Supporting Sociability. New York: Wiley, 2000.

Redfern, S. & Naughton, N., Collaborative Virtual Environments to Support Communication and Community in Internet-Based Distance Education, Journal of Information Technology Education, Vol. 1, No. 3, 201–209, 2002.

Reinhold, O. & Alt, R. (2009). Enhancing collaborative CRM with mobile technologies, 22nd Bled eConference, Enablement:Facilitating an Open, Effective and Representative eSociety, June 14–17, 2009; Bled, Slovenia.

Riemer, K. & Vehring, N. (2008). Should 'virtual' mean 'vague'? A plea for more conceptual clarity in researching virtual organisations, 21st Bled eConference Collaboration: Overcoming Boundaries Through Multi-Channel Interaction, June 15–18, 2008; Bled, Slovenia.

Sauter, C., Mühlherr, T. & Teufel, S. (1994). Sozio-kulturelle Auswirkungen von Groupware. In: Rauch, W.; Strohmeier, F.; Hiller, H.; Schlögl, C. (eds): Proc. 4 Intl. Symp. für Informationswissenschaft, Universitätsverlag Konstanz, pp. 517–526.

Stieglitz, S., Lattemann, C., vom Brocke, J. & Sonnenberg, C., Economics of Virtual Communities – A Financial Analysis of a Case Study at the Berlin Stock Exchange, 21st Bled eConference Collaboration:Overcoming Boundaries Through Multi-Channel Interaction, June 15–18, 2008; Bled, Slovenia, 2008.

Tromp, J. & Snowdon, D., Virtual Body language: providing Appropriate User Interfaces in Collaborative Virtual Environments. Proceedings ACM VRST '97, pp. 37–44, 1997.

Use of the Internet – lessons learned from studies among the young in Slovenia

Mirna Macur

National Institute of Public Health, Ljubljana, Slovenia

Abstract

Modern media, especially the Internet, play a central role in our lives, especially in the lives of the young generation; therefore, it attracts the attention of researchers, politicians and the public. The evaluation of the role of the Internet in our everyday lives is controversial. We can find many studies that stress the positive effects of media and the Internet on the development of individuals and society, because it performs so many different functions. Others find that the virtualisation of everyday life (frequent use of information technology and its increasing importance in everyday life) has negative effects on individuals and society. The focus of this article is on the young since they are the most frequent users of the Internet. Two extensive representative studies among Slovenian youth between 16 and 29 years old were conducted in 2000 and 2010 that triggered our attention. We analysed this data to learn as much as possible about those people who use the Internet most frequently and to establish if they differ from their peers. We found significant differences in the personal values of the young in 2000 in relation to the frequency of their use of the Internet. However, the results of the study in 2010 show that the young in Slovenia are a relatively homogeneous group according to their use of the Internet – not many factors seem to influence frequency of Internet use, nor are they influenced by heavy Internet use.

Keywords

young, modern media, Internet, heavy Internet use, virtualisation of everyday life, values

1. Mass media research – past and present

The mass media has long been an important research topic for various social scientists. We are all exposed to mass media whether we are aware of it or not. We listen to the radio in cars, buses and bars; television is always on in many public places and at home. We are not aware of the vast influence that mass media has on our lives and it plays a particularly important role for the young who grew up in a 'media environment'. They are also the most frequent users of 'modern' mass media such as the Internet.

The world of mass media develops fast. Can social scientists cope with such fast development or are they lagging behind? Traditional mass media studies included several broad topics of research, such as:

– Range and scope of mass media.
– Impact and influence of particular messages and particular media on their audience.
– How media organisations work and who makes them work (Dennis, 1989).

Much early media research explored the impact and effect of print media, because print has long been regarded as a permanent record of history and events. Also, the impact of films and TV commercials has been widely explored. A wide range of resources was available for this kind of research, since marketing is a large industry. Later on media research shifted from addressing specifically effects-oriented paradigms to exploring the nature of the institutions of media production themselves as well as examining the unique characteristics of each form of media. These are qualitative in nature because they take into account context-specific situations, enabling the understanding of the power and impact of media.

These three topics are of course not all possible topics of research. We should bear in mind that media are analysed by sociologists, political scientists, economists, psychologists, artists and many more. They all have a different focus – some on individuals, families or other social groups, society in general or on the structure of media organisation. In this respect we find many relevant research questions, such as: Are media unifying or fragmenting? Does media content help the socialisation process, or just the opposite? Do people feel powerless in not being able to shape the messages of the media? There are several possible questions about the relationship between media and politics. Whose interests do media serve – public interest or the interests of rich and powerful corporations? How do new media technologies change our traditional ways of communicating? (Alexander and Hanson, 2001).

Media development in the last decade has shifted areas of research drastically. We no longer have doubts about the influence of particular media and messages on audiences; we have a problem in measuring this influence because of the explosion of mass, particularly electronic, media. We live in a media-rich environment where almost everybody has access to some form of media. In Western societies people also have enormous choices in terms of content, which poses many questions about the relationships between media and individuals, and media and society. However, the relationship is not simple. Mass media have changed dramatically in recent years. "Not long ago, 'mass' media referred to messages that were created by large organizations for broad, heterogeneous audiences. This concept no longer suffices for contemporary media environment. While the 'mass' media still exist in the forms of radio, television, film, and general interest newspaper and magazines, many media forms today are hybrids of 'mass' and 'personal' media technologies that open a new realm of understanding about how audiences process the meaning of the messages. Digital technologies and distribution forms have created many opportunities for merging (or converging) media. The Internet, for example, has the capacity to transmit traditional voice, mail, text and image-based content in a unique form of instant communication while the senders of the messages may be, or appear to be, anonymous." (Alexander and Hanson, 2001: xiii).

2. Scope of our analysis

Our daily lives are consumed by the Internet, which offers many mass media services, but also transforms and reshapes some of the traditional media (telephone, television, newspapers). An important question is how individuals in society use media in a variety of formats and contexts and how they make sense of the messages they take from the content of those media forms. Mass media research nowadays is much more complex because the topics of research are more complex.

In this article we are going to focus on the Internet as a modern and fastest growing media, especially among the young. They spend a lot of time in front of computers using the Internet, e-mail and social networks of different kinds. They of course watch a lot of TV too – many believe too much. Researchers often focus on the importance of mass media in the lives of children and the young, because:

1) Young are the most frequent media users.
2) Young start to use new (electronic) media first.
3) Media changed drastically in recent years (Roberts et al., 2005).

These reasons give us many motives to investigate the young in Slovenia. Use of the Internet is one of the fastest growing areas and the young, who use it more frequently than other age groups, have a different youth from ours. The world changed drastically in the last decade. Recent studies from the United States of America and some other Western European countries report that the young spend from five to seven, and even more, hours on the Internet per day. The term *Net Generation* is definitely in place (Van der Beemt et al., 2010). Livingstone (2008) claims that the Net generation often leave parents behind without being able to follow what their children are doing on the Internet.

In Slovenia two extensive representative studies were conducted among the young from 16 to 29 years old – namely in 2000 and 2010. A random sample was selected from a central register of the population previously selected in 12 regions and 6 types of settlements. The implemented sample was corrected through a weighting process. The aim of both studies was to present in detail the young generation in Slovenia through their views on politics and democracy, values, habits, social networks, interests, ways of spending (free) time, views on school, work, family and problems of the young (Lavrič et al., 2011 and Miheljak et al., 2001).

3. Importance of new media, especially the Internet among the young in Slovenia

Use of the Internet is growing extremely quickly. The latest data from 2010 shows that 73% of the Slovenian population are Internet users; whereas about a quarter of the population still do not use the Internet. They are the ones that are primarily not interested in the use of the Internet or they don't know how to use it. Obstacles to using the Internet are more frequent among those with lower education, among the older generation (older than 60), and also women tend to use the Internet less frequently than men. In Figure 1 we find non-users and a small share of Internet ex-users. Usually, they claim they don't need it any more, most often because they are retired. Also, a lack of interest can be detected in this group as well as not having a computer or having poor knowledge of English language (Vehovar et al., 2011).

Internet use in Slovenia is above the European average (in 2011 there were 58.3% of Europeans using the Internet) but below the average use of the Internet in North America, where 78.3% of the population use the Internet (RIS: Svetovni plet, 2011).

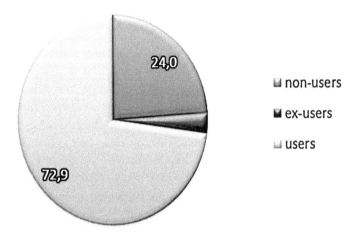

Fig. 1:   Internet use in Slovenia (Vehovar et al., 2011)

2010 data show that the young in Slovenia use the Internet much more than the rest of the population. In Figure 2 we find that most Slovenians older than 65 years have never used the Internet. Most young, however (from 10 to 34 years), use the Internet (almost) every day.

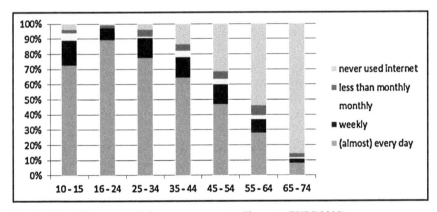

Fig. 2:   Use of Internet in different age groups in Slovenia (SURS 2010)

This trend is similar in other European countries, but the reverse used to be the case. In 2000 international research conducted by Jupiter Computers and Media Metrix showed that the Internet and computers were used by adults more than by teenagers. Teenagers accessed the Internet less frequently and spent fewer hours on the Internet than adults. Results of the study surprisingly showed that teenagers spent on average 303 minutes per month, whereas adults spent 728 minutes per month on the Internet (Jamnik, 2000). It seems that use of the Internet was heavily dependent on access to it which was not as good as it is now. Nowadays, the young, mostly, do not have problems in accessing the Internet – if not in use at home, the Internet is always available at schools and libraries. The motives for the young to use the Internet are not difficult to identify – primarily it is driven by the peer-to-peer opportunities that this new media enables. They provide opportunities for mutual responsiveness, criticism, humour, feedback, openness and networking that are so often absent from content designed for children by adults (Livingstone, 2008).

The Internet of course has negative effects for the young too; most relate to violence, harassment, illegal content on the Internet and abuse of children (Jurišić, 2009). Some protective mechanisms are developing in order to safeguard against abuse of the young, especially children, but they are not sufficiently effective. The Internet is, and remains, very popular for most teenagers.

Authors of the research among young in Slovenia in 2010 did not analyse all possible effects of heavy internet use, but they do report positive and negative effect. In relation to the use of traditional and modern media, they report:

1. 82% of the young use the Internet (almost) every day. The percentage of such users in Slovenia is above the European average EU-15 and EU-27.
2. Use of information-communication technology is not replacing face-to-face communication but is in positive correlation with such communication. The young in Slovenia also show positive correlation between use of ICT on one hand and cultural, art, humanitarian and political activities on the other.
3. The young use computers primarily for fun and communication.
4. With use of a computer for fun purposes (Internet sites for social networking, computer games) we find positive correlation with less favourable psychosocial characteristics of the young.
5. Concerning traditional media, the young follow news more than a decade ago; on the other hand, entertainment through traditional media lost popularity in this age group.

6. More frequent communication on the phone is related to the impaired psychosocial state of an individual. (Lavrič et al., 2011: 299).

4. Does heavy use of the Internet reflects on values of the young in Slovenia

Do personal values influence the use of modern technology, Internet in particular, or does heavy use of the Internet influence personal values? It seems that information specialist believe in the first interpretation, whereas social scientists (including the author) believe in the second. Western societies use mass media to impose their set of beliefs, values, knowledge and behavioural norms on other countries. This is especially evident in cultures that differ from Western societies. In Asia there is much evidence of cultural imperialism; we quote from a research among high school students in the Philippines. "The Tans reported that the students' own values – and particularly terminal values – conflicted sharply with the values they perceived in American television programs. While American programs were viewed as stressing such terminal values as 'pleasure', 'an exciting life' and 'freedom' students personally deemphasized these values in favour of 'a world at peace', 'equity' and 'true friendship'. A regression analysis revealed that American television viewing was significantly associated with 'pleasure' and negatively associated with 'salvation', 'wisdom' and 'forgiving'" (Salwen, 1991: 34).

Use of the Internet today brings even bigger changes to the young generation than television did 20 years ago. The young live not only in the natural environment but also more and more in the so-called virtual environment, which seems to be addictive. Looking around us we see young people with cell phones and computers, and they both give the young completely new forms of socialisation. "This new media and information communication environment of the young is dramatically different from the one in which their parents lived. It is apparently more accessible; it takes place in the privacy of their rooms. It is more interactive and apparently more under the influence of the young than any other environment for young and children sofar" (Ule, 2008: 197).

This gives us the motive to explore the relationships between the personal values of the young and use of the Internet in two extensive representative Slovenian studies, namely Young 2000 and Young 2010. Values include beliefs and cognitive structures that are closely related to feelings. Values are related to preferred goals (social equality, freedom, honesty) and go beyond limited circumstances and actions. Values are used as measures for selection, evaluation of actions, politics, people, institutions and their ranking among good or bad, legal or illegal, trustworthy or not – always in the direction of stated goals (Toš, 2004). Following this description we should keep in mind that most surveys on values inside social science data archives concern views on politics, government and other institutions, and often also on security. In this study we will limit the analysis to personal values; we will not analyse trust in institutions and government. These values will be compared with the frequency of using the Internet (for example average number of hours using the Internet for personal needs). This was the easiest way to compare the two groups of people (those who use the Internet frequently and those who use it seldom or never) with the help of a t-test for two independent samples. With such a test we were able to compare the value orientations of the two groups of respondents and establish if the differences between them were significant.

The study among young Slovenians (16–29 years of age) in 2000 showed that the most important values for them were health and true friendship. It was also interesting to see that the most similar answers among the young also concerned health (standard deviation of answers was the smallest). This phenomenon is typical for the Slovenian population at large; recognised in the transition period and now in a time of recession. We were however surprised to see that the young generation favoured health over other values. Usually, the young mostly favour the things they don't have over the things they do have (health does not represent such a big problem for them as, for example, a stable job or material wellbeing). Data show that health remains the most important value for Slovenians and for the young even nowadays. The least important value for the young in 2000 was 'power over other people'. The most diverse answers to different values (meaning the highest standard deviation) were attributed to 'live in peace with oneself', 'have power over the others', 'be an authority or leader', 'creativity and originality' (Miheljak et al., 2001).

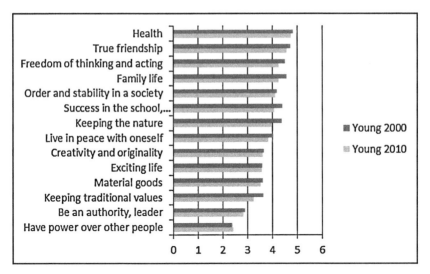

Fig. 3: Values of the young in Slovenia in 2000 and 2010 (Lavrič et al., 2010). 5-point Likert type scale was used in both studies (1 – not important at all to 5 – very important)

The values of the young in 2000 were compared with frequency of Internet use. We found some significant differences between those who used the Internet frequently and those who used the Internet seldom or never. Young people who often used the Internet believed that:

- 'Security of the nation' is less important (although on average still very important) than the ones who use the Internet seldom or never.
- 'Creativity and originality' is more important.
- 'Peace in the world without conflicts' is less important for them as it is for others.
- 'Keeping traditional values' seems to be less important for them than for the others.
- They find 'family life' less important than the others.
- 'Freedom of thinking and acting' is for the ones who often use the Internet more important than for the others (see Table 1 in Appendix).

Those who used the Internet frequently favoured creativity and freedom more, whereas those who didn't use the Internet, or used it seldom, found traditional values more important (see Table 1 in Appendix). At this point we don't know whether the Internet can be interpreted as a medium which is a value setter or if personal values determine how many hours we spend on the Internet.

Let us also consider values and frequency of Internet use among the young in the 2010 research. The values in both questionnaires were the same, but three more values were included in the 2000 questionnaire ('Security of the nation from enemies', 'Peace in the world without conflicts', 'The world of beauty, nature, art') compared to the 2010 questionnaire.

The most important value nowadays is still 'health', followed by 'true friendship', 'family life', 'freedom to act and think', 'order and stability in society', 'success in school/at work', 'protect the nature'. The least important for the young in 2010 was 'power over other people' and to 'be an authority, leader' (see Figure 3).

The values of the young were compared to the frequency of Internet use. The scale of answers was the same in both studies for values, but different for Internet use in 2000 and in 2010. In 2010 there was a numerical variable explaining how many hours per day[1] the young spent on the Internet. According to the results 34.2% of the young use the Internet for a maximum of one hour daily. On the other side of the scale, we find 17.8% of the young who use the Internet for more than three hours daily. Frequency of Internet use was compared with values of the young with the help of the Pearson correlation coefficient.

We were surprised to learn that no correlation was found between the number of hours spent on the Internet per day and the values of the young in 2010. Results from 2000 were not repeated. More importantly, no correlation between frequency of Internet use and other variables in the questionnaire were found to be at least ±0,1 strong[2]. That applies to:

- Values of young people (21 variables).
- Interest in different areas, topics (17 variables).
- Current relationship with parents (11 variables).
- Self-perception (17 variables).
- Reactions to problems (9 variables).
- Habits and indulgencies (8 variables).

---

1   Valid answers go from 8 minutes to 15 hours.
2   Results are not included in Appendix because there are too many variables included in this Correlation analysis.

- Current fears and fears for the future (11 variables).
- Satisfaction with own life (3 variables).

Results were surprising. They can be interpreted in various ways, such as:

- Internet not being a value setter, the way traditional media have presented.
- Globalisation process is so strong that use of the Internet does not represent a major factor in value shaping.
- Everybody uses the Internet so frequently that frequent use is not a relevant variable anymore.

5. Who spends a lot of time on the Internet among the young in Slovenia today?

To test these interpretations we decided to test who uses the Internet (the most) among the young population in Slovenia. We selected socio-demographic variables and compared them with frequency of Internet use. Analysis showed that Internet use among the young in 2010 *does not depend* on:

- Gender.
- Age (bearing in mind that the target population is between 15 and 29 years old).
- Education.
- Religion.
- Ownership of the place where they live.

However, we did find some variables that are connected with Internet use. Frequency of Internet use *depends on* the status ($\chi^2 = 55,42$; sig. $\chi^2 = 0,000$) in a way that:

- Those who are employed full time spend much less time on the Internet than all the others (students, pupils, unemployed, part-time employed).
- Students spend much more time on the Internet than the rest of the young.
- Pupils of technical high schools (not gymnasium) spend less time on the Internet than the rest of the young.

Frequency of Internet use also *depends on* the place where the young spent most of their life ($\chi^2 = 23,31$; sig. $\chi^2 = 0,003$):

- Those who lived in big cities (over 100,000) and those who lived in smaller cities (between 10,000 and 50,000) spent more time on the Internet than others.
- Those who lived in the countryside spent much less time on the Internet than others.

Frequency of Internet use also *depends on* the place where the young live now ($\chi^2 = 30,61$; sig. $\chi^2 = 0,000$):

- Those who live in big cities (over 100,000) and those who live in smaller cities (between 10,000 and 50,000) spend more time on the Internet than others.
- Those who live in the countryside spend much less time on the Internet than others.

6. Discussion

We were surprised to learn that there is such a small number of variables connected with frequency of Internet use in our newest data, gathered from the young in 2010. First of all, no connection between values and frequency of Internet use can be found. Also, other interests and aspirations of the young in Slovenia nowadays cannot be explained by heavy Internet use. Data indicate that minimal use of the Internet is due to the lack of time among the full-time employed and those living in villages compared to the others.

10 years ago digital divide[3] was measured in Slovenia according to access to the Internet – significant differences in time spent on the Internet were identified in numerous socio-demographic variables, such as age, gender, social strata, type of living (urban/rural), religion and income. Reasons for not using the Internet were different in different population groups but the main message of the report was that digital divide in recent years has not been diminishing but was strengthening, especially according to age, education and income (Dolničar et al., 2002).

Access to the Internet in 2012 does not seem to be the problem – at least not for the young generation. Study among the young in 2010 shows that values

---

3 Digital divide refers to individuals, households, companies and regions according to access to information communication technologies (ICT) and their use.

and time are what determine how long people stay on the Internet and not vice versa. Also, place of living seems to be a value setter. T-test among two independent groups: living in big cities / living in the countryside showed that:

- Those living in the countryside respect traditional values more – significant differences are shown in values: 'order and stability in a society', 'keeping traditional values', 'family life' and 'protect the nature'.
- Those living in big cities have more modern values: 'exciting life', 'material goods', 'living in peace with oneself'.

Overall, it seems that lifestyle is what determines the frequency of Internet use and not vice versa, which is presented in Figure 4. We also draw two assumptions, derived from the literature and not from the data available. Internet addiction is a term that is used in professional and public debate more and more but the meaning of the term is still unclear. We can agree on the fact that heavy use of the Internet triggers it but we cannot know how much use of the Internet is too much. Addiction theory does not stress so much the number of hours on the Internet as much as other addiction indicators – brain and emotional reaction to 'not having Internet' is similar to other addictions (alcohol and drugs for example). Some experts warn that intensity of Internet use is too high, especially among the young. In Slovenia data on Internet addiction is not available, but data on gambling addiction among high school pupils in two Slovenian regions are. The School of Applied Social Studies, in 2010, conducted a study among pupils of higher classes of secondary schools in Goriška and Dolenjska. A five times higher proportion of pathological gamblers[4] among pupils in Goriška was found in comparison with the Slovenian average, and an eight times higher proportion of pathological gamblers among pupils of Dolenjska than the Slovenian average (Igranje na srečo, 2010). Internet addiction is not the same as gambling addiction but they are related. We hope that Internet addiction is not such a big problem in Slovenia, but the results of the latest studies are not reassuring.

---

4   According to SOGS test they scored more than 4.

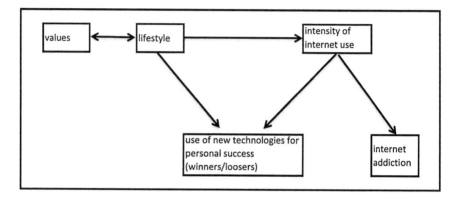

Fig. 4:   *Factors that seem to determine intensity of Internet use*

It seems everybody uses the Internet, the young in particular. The Internet brings many favourable possibilities, such as peer-to-peer communication, openness, networking and identifying new possibilities in private and professional life. However, it seems that not everybody is equally successful in so doing. Experts warn that some young people are very successful in gaining new acquaintances, friends, jobs and projects, whereas others can't successfully cope with that and show more negative effects of Internet use. We cannot empirically test this with the data available, but this dilemma remains our concern as researchers and as teachers.

Bibliography

Alexander, Alison, Hanson, Jarice (eds.): *Taking Sides: Clashing Views on Controversial Issues in Mass Media and Society*. 6th edition, McGraw-Hill/Dushkin, 2001.

Dennis Everette E: *Reshaping the Media. Mass Communication in an Information Age*, Newbury Park: Sage Publications, 1989.

Dolničar, Vesna, Kronegger, Luka, Vehovar Vasja, Vukčevič, Katja: Dogotalni razkorak v Sloveniji, Ljubljana: Fakulteta za družbene vede, 2002. http://www.ris.org/db/17/233/ Publikacije/Digitalni_razkorak_v_Sloveniji/?q=digitalnirazkorak&qdb=17&qsort=0, downloaded June 26, 2012.

Igranje na srečo med dijaki višjih letnikov srednjih šol. Primerjava med Goriško in Dolenjsko regijo, Nova Gorica: Fakulteta za uporabne družbene študije, May 2010, http:// www.fuds.si/si/dejavnosti/raziskovanje/?v=igralniske_studije, downloaded June 26, 2012.

Jamnik, Marko: Mladi in Internet. Mladina, 17. 10. 2000. http://www.mladina.si/95863/mladi-in-internet/, downloaded June 26, 2012.

Jurišić, Sanda: Percepcija uporabe Internet med mladostniki. Diplomsko delo. Fakulteta za družbene vede, Univerza v Ljubljani, 2009.

Lavrič, Miran in skupina: Mladina 2010: Družbeni profil mladih v Sloveniji [datoteka podatkov]. Slovenija, Maribor: Univerza v Mariboru, Filozofska fakulteta [izdelava], 2010. Slovenija, Ljubljana: Univerza v Ljubljani, Arhiv družboslovnih podatkov [distribucija], 2011. Lavrič, M., Flere, S., Tavčar Krajnc, M., Klanjšek, R., Musli, B., Naterer, A., Kirbiš, A., Divjak, M., Lešek, P.: Mladina 2010. Družbeni profil mladih v Sloveniji. Maribor: Aristej, 2011. http://www.adp.fdv.uni-lj.si/opisi/mla10/, downloaded May 5, 2012

Livingstone, Sonja: "Internet Literacy. Young People's Negotiation of New Online Opportunities". In PcPherson, Tara (ed.): *Digital Youth, Innovation, and the Unexpected*. Cambridge: The MIT Press, 2008.

Miheljak, Vlado, Mirjana Ule, Tanja Rener, Metka Mencin Čeplak, Blanka Tivadar in Metka Kuhar: Mladina, 2000 [datoteka podatkov]. Ljubljana: Fakulteta za družbene vede. Center za socialno psihologijo [izdelava], 2000. Ljubljana: Univerza v Ljubljani. Arhiv družboslovnih podatkov [distribucija], februar 2001. http://www.adp.fdv.uni-lj.si/opisi/mla00/, downloaded Maj 15, 2012.

RIS: Svetovni splet 2011. http://www.ris.org/db/26/9530/Novice/Svetovni_splet_/, downloaded June 23, 2012.

Roberts, D. F., Foehr, U. G., Rideout, V.: Generation M: media in the lives of 8–18 year olds. Menlo Park CA: Kaiser Family Foundation, 2005.

Salwen, Michael B : *Cultural Imperialism: A Media Effects Approach. Critical Studies in Mass Communication,* 8 (1991), 29–38.

Statistični Urad Republike Slovenije (SURS). http://www.stat.si/, downloaded June 23, 2012.

Toš, Niko: *Beležka o vrednotah*. Pogovori o prihodnosti Slovenije pri predsedniku republike Slovenije. 2, O vrednotah. Ljubljana, 2004.

Ule, Mirjana: *Spremembe vrednot v sodobnih družbah novih tveganj in negotovosti.* Pogovori o prihodnosti Slovenije pri predsedniku republike Slovenije. 2, O vrednotah. Ljublja na, 2004.

Van den Beemt, A., Akkerman, S., Simons, R. S.: The use of interactive media among today's youth: results of a survey. *Computers in Human Behaviour,* 26, 1158–1165, 2010.

Vehovar, Vasja, Činkole Tina, Prevodnik, Katja: Digitalni razkorak 2010. RIS – Raba Internet v Sloveniji. Ljubljana, maj 2011. http://www.ris.org/db/13/12069/RIS%20poročila/Digitalni_razkorak_2010/?&p1=276&p2=285&p3=1318, downloaded June 23, 2012.

Appendix

Table 1: Values of the young (16 to 29 years old) in 2000 compared with Internet use

	Use of Internet	N	Mean	Std. Devia-tion	Std. Error Mean	T statistics	Sig. t
True friend-ship	Never, seldom	637	4,74	,542	,021	-1,313	0,190
	often	415	4,78	,469	,023		
The world of beauty, nature, art	Never, seldom	637	3,87	,899	,036	-1,865	0,063
	often	415	3,98	,911	,045		
Health	Never, seldom	637	4,82	,470	,019	0,128	0,371
	often	415	4,80	,474	,023		
Order and stability in a society	Never, seldom	637	4,20	,755	,030	1,327	0,185
	often	415	4,14	,812	,040		
Exciting life	Never, seldom	634	3,62	,939	,037	-0,097	0,923
	often	415	3,62	,965	,047		
Material goods	Never, seldom	637	3,61	,946	,037	1,308	0,191
	often	415	3,54	,897	,044		
Security of the nation from enemies	Never, seldom	636	**4,24**	,939	,037	2,503	**0,012**
	often	414	**4,09**	,945	,046		
Success in the school, profession	Never, seldom	637	4,45	,728	,029	1,098	0,272
	often	415	4,40	,704	,035		
Creativity and originality	Never, seldom	635	**3,67**	,945	,038	-3,990	**0,000**
	often	415	**3,91**	,956	,047		

	Use of Internet	N	Mean	Std. Deviation	Std. Error Mean	T statistics	Sig. t
Peace in the world without conflicts	Never, seldom	636	**4,53**	,794	,031	2,974	**0,003**
	often	415	**4,38**	,864	,042		
Keeping traditional values	Never, seldom	635	**3,69**	,983	,039	3,288	**0,001**
	often	415	**3,49**	,963	,047		
Family life	Never, seldom	636	**4,64**	,676	,027	4,949	**0,000**
	often	415	**4,40**	,831	,041		
Keeping the nature	Never, seldom	635	4,39	,809	,032	0,460	0,645
	often	415	4,37	,713	,035		
Be an authority, leader	Never, seldom	634	2,89	1,041	,041	-1,007	0,314
	often	415	2,96	1,062	,052		
Have power over other people	Never, seldom	635	2,39	1,054	,042	-0,020	0,984
	often	415	2,39	1,102	,054		
Live in peace with oneself	Never, seldom	634	4,04	1,180	,047	-0,294	0,769
	often	415	4,07	1,089	,053		
Freedom of thinking and acting	Never, seldom	635	**4,49**	,763	,030	-2,925	**0,004**
	often	415	**4,62**	,674	,033		

Source: Miheljak et al., 2001.

The average value was calculated by using the scale from 1 – 'not important at all' to 5 – 'very important'.

Perceived effects of web classrooms in primary schools in Slovenia

Andi Jambrošić

Primary school Metlika and Primary school Podzemelj, Slovenia

Blaž Rodič

Faculty of information studies in Novo mesto, Slovenia

Abstract

This contribution presents our research on the effects of web classrooms on the education process in Slovenia's primary schools. ICT has become a crucial teaching tool in the development of the information society. Primary schools in Slovenia follow the developments in e-learning, and have largely introduced web-based e-learning and distance education in the past few years. We have gathered the data from teachers and pupils using web based questionnaires and analysed it with statistical tools. The results indicate that among other positive effects the use of web classrooms can also bring an improvement in the grades of pupils.

Keywords
e-learning, e-classrooms, primary schools, Moodle

1. Introduction

Most primary schools in Slovenia have recently adopted web classrooms as a supplementary platform for teaching. Web classrooms implemented in Moodle and similar environments present opportunities for enhancement of the education process, and research (Brečko and Vehovar, 2008) has shown that e-learning can lead to increased pupils motivation, increased data handling abilities and the ability of pupils to adjust their learning pace.

New methods of ICT use in education has been well received by the pupils, which are considered to be well versed in general use of ICT, as well as by their teachers (Brečko, 2010). Web classrooms have enabled the teachers to expand the methods of collaboration with pupils, to easily publish content, and better connect different courses through easier access to the materials and information from other courses and simplified exchange of ideas and experiences among teachers (Potočar and Ignaz 2010). According to Makuc (2003), today it's compulsory to design digital versions of the teaching materials and support them with instructions and electronic tests, and make them available on the web. This brings advantages both to pupils, who can study from home, and teachers, as the new communication channels allow further support for teaching and knowledge verification.

Research has shown that the use of electronic materials has brought several positive effects on the education process (Brečko and Vehovar, 2008) and the academic achievement of pupils in Slovenia's primary schools (Šerbec, 2009).

The purpose of our research was to establish the influence of web classroom utilization on the academic achievements of pupils at primary schools in Slovenia according to the opinions of teacher and pupils and the relationship between intensity of web classroom use and its positive effects.

2. Methodology

The sample and the research method

Quantitative research has been conducted among the primary schools in the Republic of Slovenia, with the target population including all 785 primary schools and department schools (Evidenca vzgojno-izobraževalnih zavodov in vzgojno-izobraževalnih programov, 2011). The research was conducted within the classes in the third trimester (years 6 to 9), and segmented in two parts: the teachers of the third trimester, with the target population of 7,123 individuals, differentiated by the demographical qualities: age, gender, work experience, place of residence and course field, and the pupils of the third trimester, with the target population of 53,485 pupils, differentiated by their gender, age, academic achievements and place of birth (according to the SI-Stat data portal (according to the SI-Stat data portal, 2011). We have measured the opinions of teachers and pupils on the usage of web classrooms in the education process.

The research data was obtained with anonymous web questionnaires using Google Documents and Google Sites: two types of questionnaires were prepared, one for teachers and one for pupils. Both questionnaires contain closed questions, start with demographic questions, and continue with questions regarding the frequency of ICT use and the opinions of teachers and pupils regarding the influence of web classroom use on academic achievements of pupils. A five point Likert scale was used with values ranging from "1 – I completely disagree" to "5 – I completely agree".

3. Analysis of web classroom use in primary schools

Research goals and hypotheses

Web questionnaires were used to obtain data from the teachers and pupils using web classrooms in primary schools. Data was analysed to determine the influence of web classroom use on the quality of education process, motivation of pupils, and communication between teachers and pupils and, most important, the academic achievement of pupils. We have postulated several research questions about the positive effects of web classrooms on the education process. The research questions that we will focus on in this paper are:

• Do web classrooms improve the pupils' motivation to learn?
• Do web classrooms improve the academic achievement of pupils?

Demographic data

Teachers

Of the 7,123 teachers in the target population, 474 (6.65%) responded to the questionnaire. Of the interviewed teachers 21.10% are male and 78.90% female, which corresponds with the statistical data on the target population – the teachers of the third trimester (20.65% males according to the SI-Stat data portal (according to the SI-Stat data portal, 2011). The age of the teachers' ranges from approximately 32 years to 50 years, and their work experience ranges from 6.89 to 27.75 years, meaning that different groups of teachers, with a wide spectrum of age and work experience are present in the sample.

Pupils

Of the 53,485 pupils in the target population, 1,072 (2%) have responded to the questionnaire. Of the pupils, 48.60% were male and 51.60% were female, which corresponds with the statistical data on the target population (according to the SI-Stat data portal, 2011). The age of pupils was between 11.57 years and 13.89 years.

Analysis of ICT use and web classroom use

Teachers

The scale of ICT usage frequency we used was "never", "sometimes", "several times per month", "frequently", "very frequently". The research has shown that teachers "very frequently" use computers to search for data on the web (82.28%), browse the web (76.37%), prepare documents and presentations (75.95%) and prepare exams for pupils (69.41%).

Less frequently, teachers use the computers to communicate with pupils (47.25% do it "sometimes", and 21.10% "never" do it). This is expected, as computer based communication with pupils is seldom needed.

Teachers use web classrooms quite often, as 22.36% use them "several times per month", while 41.14% use them "frequently" or "very frequently".

Opinion on web classrooms

Few of the participating teachers disagreed with the statements about the advantages of web classrooms. The less agreed with statements were that the web classrooms raise the academic achievements of pupils (rated 1 – "I completely disagree" by 6.54% and rated 2 by 20.04%), and that the web classrooms make work with academically challenged pupils easier (rated 1 by 6.75% and rated 2 by 27%).

Table 1.1 also shows that the biggest perceived advantages of web classrooms are easier access to teaching materials and allowing additional consolidation of knowledge and study of materials, and the advantages that follow are the communication with pupils, knowledge verification, better teaching of the gifted pupils and better motivation of pupils to learn.

Table 1.1: Evaluation of teachers' opinions of the advantages of web classrooms

How much do you agree with the following statements on advantages of web classrooms.	Arithmetic mean	Standard deviation	Range of opinion	
			From	To
Easier access to additional materials.	4.16	0.93	3.23	5
Allow additional consolidation of knowledge and study.	4.14	0.89	3.25	5
Additional possibilities for communication between teachers and pupils.	3.96	0.99	2.97	4.95

How much do you agree with the following statements on advantages of web classrooms.	Arithmetic mean	Standard deviation	Range of opinion From	To
Additional activities for knowledge verification.	3.90	0.98	2.92	4.88
Better teaching of gifted pupils.	3.88	0.97	2.91	4.85
Increase pupils motivation to learn	3.65	1.00	2.65	4.65
Enables linking of courses	3.64	0.92	2.72	4.56
Enables connection of materials with other courses	3.54	0.93	2.61	4.47
Increase general quality of teaching process	3.48	1.01	2.47	4.49
Easier to follow progress of pupils	3.21	1.08	2.13	4.29
Easier work with academically challenged pupils	3.00	1.07	1.93	4.07
Better academic achievements (grades)	2.96	0.92	2.04	3.88

Pupils

Pupils use ICT very often to communicate with friends (56.44%), search for data (46.36%) and browse the web (44.40%), also very few of them never engage in these activities. Slightly less frequently, i.e. several times per month or more often they share personal files (64.55), email files (56.06%) and use Wikis (50.37%).

At least occasionally the pupils use ICT to exchange school related files (78.26%), use web classrooms (77.14%), use forums (74.07%), prepare for exams (86.85%) and write documents (93.10%). 57.93% at least occasionally use ICT to communicate with teachers, however many (42.07%) never use ICT for that purpose.

Table 1.2 shows that the standard deviation of opinions on advantages of web classrooms of surveyed pupils was higher than that of the teachers. The biggest perceived advantages were additional consolidation of knowledge and study, additional activities for knowledge verification, and easier access to additional materials, similar to the opinions of teachers. The difference in opinions of pupils and teachers were in the better academic achievements (grades), where pupils rated the statement higher, and Additional possibilities for communication between teachers and pupils, where pupils rated the statement lower.

Table 1.2: Evaluation of pupils' opinions of the advantages of web classrooms

How much do you agree with the following statements on advantages of web classrooms.	Arithmetic mean	Standard deviation	Range of opinion From	Range of opinion To
Allow additional consolidation of knowledge and study.	4.01	1.16	2.85	5
Additional activities for knowledge verification.	3.93	1.16	2.77	5
Easier access to additional materials.	3.88	1.21	2.67	5
Better academic achievements (grades)	3.59	1.26	2.33	4.85
Enables connection of materials with other courses	3.57	1.23	2.34	4.80
Increase pupils motivation to learn	3.47	1.32	2.15	4.79
Additional possibilities for communication between teachers and pupils.	3.45	1.25	2.20	4.70
Increase general quality of teaching process	3.35	1.20	2.15	4.55

We have noticed that the few of the surveyed use web classrooms daily (17.93% of teachers and 7.46% of pupils), however many use them occasionally or more often (93.25% of teachers and 77.14% of pupils).

Answering the research questions

Several tests of relevant variables were conducted and compared to get a statistically reliable answer to the research questions.

The first research question is: **Do web classrooms improve the pupils' motivation to learn?**

Table 1.3 shows that the opinions of teachers and pupils are very similar. In average, the surveyed weakly agree with the statement that web classrooms improve the pupils' motivation to learn. From the confidence limits we can conclude that the surveyed weakly agree that the web classrooms improve the pupils' motivation to learn.

Table 1.3: Numeric values and the t-test for the first research question

	Arithmetic mean	Standard deviation	Asymmetry	Flatness	95 % confidence interval Lower value	95 % confidence interval Upper value
Teachers	3.65	1.00	-0.46	-0.20	3.56	3.74
Pupils	3.47	1.32	-0.41	-0.97	3.39	3.55

The variable on increase of pupil motivation was compared with the variable of web classroom usage frequency as we wanted to show the difference in opinions relatively to the usage frequency.

Levene's test of variance homogeneity:

- Statistical significance (Pr) – teachers = 0.47
- Statistical significance (Pr) – pupils = 2.03e-12

As the result of Levene's test of variance homogeneity for the variable in the case of teachers is bigger than 0.05, the hypothesis on variance homogeneity is valid and one way analysis of variance can be performed. However, for pupils the result is less than 0.05, therefore the hypothesis on variance homogeneity is not valid, and a different test was performed for this variable – the Kruskal-Wallis test.

Table 1.4: One way analysis of variance and the Kruskal-Wallis test for the first research question

	Teachers (one way variance test)			Pupils (Kruskal-Wallis)	
	Arithmetic mean	Standard deviation	Statistical significance	Rank	Statistical significance
Never	3.29	1.06		3	
Sometimes	3.51	1.00		3	
Several times per month	3.64	0.85	8.25e-8	4	2.2e-16
Frequently	3.71	0.92		4	
Very frequently	4.21	0.95		5	

The results of both tests (see Table 1.4) have shown similar values, thus we can conclude that both groups (teachers and pupils) share similar opinions. Those that use web classrooms think that they increase the motivation of pupils to learn, and higher usage frequency corresponds with higher opinion on the web classrooms effect on pupil motivation. Those that use web classrooms very frequently completely agree with the statement that web classrooms improve the pupils' motivation to learn. Statistical significance of both tests is under 0.05 thus we can conclude that above statements are valid for the entire primary school population.

According to the findings above, we can answer the research question: Both the teacher and the pupil populations weakly agree that the web classrooms improve the pupils' motivation to learn.

The second research question was: **Do web classrooms improve the academic achievement of pupils?**

Table 1.5 shows that the opinions of surveyed teachers and pupils do not differ a lot, and that the difference is close to the threshold of agreement (below 3: no agreement, above 3: agreement). In average, teachers are neutral towards the statement in hypothesis. The value is slightly below the threshold of agreement, and the standard deviation is nearly 1, meaning that there are two significant groups present: some teachers agree with the statement, and others don't. From the standard deviation we can conclude that a similar dissonance is also present in the population of pupils.

Table 1.5: Numeric values and the t-test for the second research question

Variable	Arithmetic mean	Standard deviation	Asymmetry	Flatness	95 % confidence interval	
					Lower value	Higher value
Teachers	2.96	0.92	- 0.05	0.05	2.88	3.04
Pupils	3.59	1.26	- 0.52	- 0.75	3.51	3.67

The variable on increase of academic achievements of pupils was compared with the variable of web classroom usage frequency, as we wanted to show the difference in opinions relatively to the usage frequency.

Levene's test of variance homogeneity:

• Statistical significance (Pr) – teachers = 0.61
• Statistical significance (Pr) – pupils = 0.00038

As the result of Levene's test of variance homogeneity for the variable in the case of teachers is bigger than 0.05, the hypothesis on variance homogeneity is valid and one way analysis of variance can be performed. However, for pupils the result is less than 0.05, therefore the hypothesis on variance homogeneity is not valid, and the Kruskal- Wallis test was performed for this variable.

Table 1.6: *One way analysis of variance and the Kruskal-Wallis test for the second research question*

	Teachers (one way variance test)			Pupils (Kruskal-Wallis)	
	Arithmetic mean	Standard deviation	Statistical significance	Standard deviation	Statistical significance
Never	2.68	0.88		3.0	
Sometimes	2.82	0.86		4.0	
Several times per month	2.92	0.90	7.42e-6	4.0	3.11e-7
Frequently	3.10	0.90		4.0	
Very frequently	3.39	0.97		4.5	

According to the one way analysis of variance for teachers (Table 1.6) it's evident that those surveyed teachers that use the web classrooms frequently or very frequently, believe that web classroom usage can improve the academic achievements of pupils, while other teachers disagree, however the values are close to the threshold of agreement. The surveyed pupils agreed with the statement much more though, as all pupils that use the web classrooms at least sometimes either agreed or strongly agreed. As the statistical significance for both groups' results is lower than 0.05, we can generalize that these results represent the entire population.

According to the findings above, we can answer the second research question: pupils tend to weakly agree that web classrooms improve the academic achievement of pupils, while teachers that use web classrooms often are neutral on this question, and teachers that rarely use web classrooms are more sceptic about the influence of web classrooms on the academic achievements of pupils.

4. Discussion

Research was aimed at e-learning, specifically the use of web classrooms in the teaching process in primary schools in Slovenia. To our knowledge this was the most comprehensive research on the use and effects of web classrooms in Slovenia's primary schools so far.

E-learning has more than ten years of history in Slovenia's schools, where it has been first adopted by higher education and secondary schools, and somewhat later by the primary schools. Perhaps the best-known current project in this field is the "E- šolstvo" (E-schools) where a public-private partnership is organising courses for teachers to raise their e-learning competences. A web community "Slovensko izobraževalno omrežje" (Slovenian education network) is a part of this project. As e-classrooms were established in most primary schools several years ago, their novelty should not have a significant influence on the motivation of pupils.

Research results indicate that both teachers and pupils perceive a positive effect on pupil's motivation to learn, which is encouraging. However the perceived effect is weak, and more could be done to motivate the pupils and make learning a fun process. Furthermore, teachers tend to be either neutral or sceptic towards the effect of web classrooms on pupil's academic achievements, while pupils in average see a weak positive effect. That can be interpreted in several ways. Perhaps teachers lack the tools and data to monitor the pupils' grades in relation to web classroom use, or the web classrooms don't really improve the results of teaching. Due to a more positive attitude of pupils, who presumably more accurately perceive the positive effects of web classrooms on their absorption and retention of knowledge we are optimistic in this regard.

An additional challenge to the teachers and developers of e-learning materials is the early exposure of pupils to ICT via their interaction with mobile phones, tablets and other technology at home, which can increase the childrens' skills and affect their expectations regarding e-learning. New e-learning courses should be developed using new paradigms (e.g. mobile gaming) and verified using methodologies such as discussed in Fong-Ling et. al (2009).

Web classrooms and ICT are now a common part of the education process in primary schools, and their positive effects are evident, but to fully use their advantages to improve the quality of our primary schools and most of all the development of pupils into knowledgeable and inquisitive young individuals, we should also focus on the development of interesting, interactive and multimedia enhanced teaching materials and their nationwide access. The development of such teaching materials should be the theme of nationwide initiatives in the future, while the focus of our future research will be on the key qualities of interactive and multimedia enhanced teaching materials for the transfer of knowledge and acceptance by both pupils and teachers.

Bibliography

Brečko, Barbara Neža and Vehovar, Vasja: Informacijska-komunikacijska tehnologija pri poučevanju in učenju v slovenskih šolah, Ljubljana, 2008.

Brečko, Barbara Neža: Uporaba računalnika med osnovnošolci, Kranjska gora, 2010.

Evidenca vzgojno-izobraževalnih zavodov in vzgojno-izobraževalnih programov, https://krka1.mss.edus.si/registriweb/Default.aspx, 2011.

Fong-Ling Fu, Rong-Chang Su, Sheng-Chin Yu, EGameFlow: A scale to measure learners' enjoyment of e-learning games, Computers & Education, Volume 52, Issue 1, ppg. 101–112, 2009.

Makuc, Alenka: Izobraževanje na daljavo s pomočjo IKT v osnovni in srednji šoli, Kranj, Organizacija, let. 32, št. 8–9, str.: 501–503, 1999.

Potočar, Zdenko in Ignaz, Lorena: Podpora skupinskemu delu na projektu v okviru spletne učilnice, Kranj, 2010.

SI-Stat podatkovni portal, http://pxweb.stat.si/pxweb/Dialog/Saveshow.asp, 2011.

Slovensko izobraževalno omrežje, http://www.sio.si, 2011.

Šerbec, Lučka Lazarev: E-izobraževanje v osnovni šoli prednosti in slabosti, Ljubljana, 2009.

Perspectives of Social Media Analytics Application in Higher Education in Serbia

Olivera Grljević, Laslo Šereš, Ružica Debeljački

Faculty of Economics Subotica, University of Novi Sad, Serbia

Abstract

The paper presents the research conducted with the idea of profiling the online behavior of students of Faculty of Economics Subotica, to investigate possibilities of sentiment analysis application in order to identify an overall sentiment about the Faculty, provided courses, and to improve general relations with students. Taking into account the new online culture that is omnipresent in the everyday behavior of students, the survey sought to identify a profile of students, to better understand their online behavior and their habits and preferences in the use of social media sites. Special emphasis is placed on usage of social media sites for education and training, furthermore on the manner and frequency of use of each social media site, as well as the popularity of particular social media as a guideline for future data sources for sentiment analysis.

Keywords

Social Media Analytics, Higher Education, Online Student Profiling

1. Introduction

A large number of online users of social media websites (social networking sites, wikis, social bookmarks, social ranking sites, sites for sharing photos and videos, etc.) constantly multiply and add information about events, services, products and experiences through various Internet platforms. With qualitative intelligent analysis (based on methods and techniques of data mining) of these contents, companies can take advantage of new data sources to get closer to their customers, develop competitive advantages and grow their business. Analogous to this, both former and present students exchange information about faculty on forums, Facebook pages, other social media sites, about course they attended, exams taken, experiences and about general impression of the faculty. Therefore, colleges and universities as service providers should also undertake social media analysis to comprehend the reputation of their institution, get familiar with the opinions of users of their services, students preferences and attitudes, so they could improve relationships with students and make an offer tailored to what students really expect to get.

Starting point of the research presented in the paper is reflected in the idea that the behavior of students on social media sites can generate potentially useful information. Analysis of such data collection can provide the answer to many questions. Do students with their comments and content generated on social media sites can influence the thinking of other students and consequently lead to favoring certain courses, and the selection of certain subjects? Do students generate content that can affect the reputation of the institution? Does the analysis of such content can identify business problems of the institution, bottlenecks or potential ideas for improvement? The goal is to examine possibilities and benefits of social media analytics in domain of higher education, as well as to lay the foundation for improving relations with the students by answering these questions.

In order to answer some of the posed questions, the initial step of the research concerned the identification of profiles of students' online behavior and examination of their current behavior. This task was conducted by surveying students of Faculty of Economics Subotica. Prior to that a pilot study was conducted in high school in order to identify problematic questions and to discuss possible alternatives, to reconsider the order of questions and their formulation, to estimate the length of the survey, to collect the opinions and suggestions of the respondents in order to improve the questionnaire, and form its final version. Data collected through a pilot study was preliminary analyzed in order to review whether the planned techniques can identify regularities in the behavior of students on social media sites. This paper presents the results of a pilot study.

Since the amount of data on the Internet is large and dispersed, and the fact that sentiment analysis involves many steps and is time consuming (Salvetti et al., 2004), (Casto et al., 2008), this study should also create guidelines for the implementation of sentiment analysis in higher education in Serbia, notably the Faculty of Economics Subotica, in terms of identifying social media sites where students produce the most relevant content (exchange views on faculty, courses, and other aspects of their education).

Presented paper is structured as follows. Chapter related work presents research conducted on a related topic which was a starting point for the research presented in this paper. Next chapter illustrates exploratory findings of a pilot study conducted with a goal of improving the survey and initial analysis of the data collected. Future research sets the future research directions and points out the limitations of the current research that has to be overcome, followed by conclusion.

2. Related Work

Due to the large amount of unfiltered information on the Internet, a major challenge for every company, regardless of the business domain, is the issue of data processing and their transformation into useful knowledge and intelligence which could improve their business. Social Media Analytics (SMA), which is most often related to the sentiment analysis and opinion mining, can contribute to this.

Sentiment analysis assesses opinion interwoven within the content generated by users with the aim of identifying true attitudes, opinions or emotional state of the writer (Pang and Lee, 2008). As pointed out in (HP, 2012) this task is extremely difficult because the feelings and emotions are subject to interference; sentiment is hardly expressed in the form of all or nothing, because it includes the range of emotions and sounds – for example, by setting the qualitative mark like "I agree completely" on the survey a true quantitative measure of what the respondent really feels will not be provided; measuring sentiment is closely associated with the content – for example, the analysis of book reviews introduces subjectivity into the analysis because the analysis is reduced to only the positive and negative responses – this analysis should also include mining based on relevance and subjectivity; sentiment can be measured in the document, paragraph, sentence, phrase, or any combination thereof.

Although numerous studies on the use of social media at the universities are carried out, particularly in the U.S. market, none of them (according to our knowledge) reflected the question of sentiment analysis application. Most examine the ways in which students use social networks and analyze correlation between their social network behavior and a certain dependent variable for instance college positive outcome, as well as its usage by faculty staff. The following of this section presents an overview of some of the conducted researches that prompted research presented in this paper.

Research conducted by Ologie about making digital connections in higher education (Ologie, 2012), reviewed ways people use social media in general and at colleges and universities. As study shows, Americas colleges and universities have been early adopters of social media and they out-blog the business world: for instance, in 2008 13% of fortunate 500 companies used blogs,

39% of Inc. 500 companies used blogs, while 41% of colleges and universities did the same. The results showed that private schools have been much faster in adopting social communication than public schools.

Through extensive use of blogs and forums on American faculties, a large amount of content is produced that could be analyzed and potentially could result in improvement of relationships with students and business of higher education institution. In the research presented in (Ologie, 2012) has not been explicitly written about the topic of blogs and forums, therefore the question of quality of that content, its informativeness, and connection to the business of a faculty, services and facilities it provides is posed.

However, research of Ologie agency has motivated examination of students' interest for writing blogs, commenting on blogs and forums. Thus generated contents are very valuable in terms of social media analysis, since through writing blogs and participating in forums people express their opinions and views on a given subject which can reveal the sentiment of visitors, as well as additional valuable information which can identify the problems, difficulties, or positive aspects of the business (brand, institutions, products, services).

Research presented in (Martin, 2012) examined whether there is a correlation between heavy usage of social media and grades, and oscillations in active social media usage over time. The research shows that there is no correlation between the amount of time students spend using social media and their grades. Grades followed similar distributions for all colleges, with the majority of students earning A's and B's. The study showed that more students use Facebook and YouTube than any other social media platform. Blogs, Twitter, MySpace, and LinkedIn had significantly lower number of users among students.

Research presented in (Pearson Learning Solutions, 2010) revealed social media sites faculty stuff use for personal communication, professional use and teaching. Majority of employees use Facebook and Youtube for personal purposes. Even 90% of employees engage in social media as part of work and up to 78% of faculty members use at least one social media in support of their professional career activities, especially YouTube and Facebook, while for teaching purposes 80% of faculty members use social media for some aspect of a course that they are teaching; nearly two-thirds use social media within their class session, and 30% post content for students to view outside of class session.

The goal of the research presented in (Junco, 2011) was to answer questions about possible relationship between the frequency of Facebook use and Facebook activities and a) student engagement (measured in several ways), b) time spent preparing for class, and c) time spent in co-curricular activities. Results indicate that Facebook use was significantly negatively predictive of engagement scale score and positively predictive of time spent in co-curricular activities. Additionally, some Facebook activities were positively predictive of the dependent variables (for instance, commenting on content and creating or RSVP'ing to events), while others were negatively predictive (for instance, frequency of playing games and checking up on friends).

Since the goal of the research presented in this paper is to examine and explore the habits and behavior of students in social media sites that could indicate the necessity of applying analytical methods and techniques in this domain, the analysis of the research presented in (Junco, 2011), (Martin, 2012), (Ologie, 2012) pointed out the necessity of analysis of usage frequency of certain social media sites, as well as the ways of their usage for personal and educational purposes. In addition, we identified activities that can be considered as motivators to connect through social media sites, and the same number of entertainment activities and activities that are closely related to education and school/academic activities were included in the questionnaire for this purpose.

By analyzing the obtained data not only the reasons of students' social networking can be better understood, but also different profiles of students can be identified. There is an obvious influence of social media and networks in all aspects of life and business that led inevitably to the profile changes of the average consumer, and analogously students. Analysis of habits and behavior profiles of students in an online environment also presents a roadmap for inclusion of social media sites in the educational process. This would allow higher education institutions to adapt to the changed profile of the average student and adjust certain aspects of their business to the demands and habits of students.

Motivated by presented research, the research was conducted at Faculty of Economics Subotica in order to identify online student profiles which will shade a light on their social media sites behavior, how they use it, how often, which social media sites are most popular, which of them are commonly used for purposes of education, do they use social media sites solely for entertainment or for professional and educational purposes also. These findings should set direction for further research, as well as the directions for the search of content on the Internet that will present the input for social media analytics, particularly sentiment analysis.

3. Exploratory findings of a pilot study

As pointed out throughout the paper, the main objective of conducted research is to examine behavioral patterns of students in an online environment in order to generate their profiles, to set directions for future research goals, and to set the baseline for social media analytics application, notably sentiment analysis. The methodology of conducted research involved: definition of survey questions; creation of survey; pilot study and processing of obtained data; surveying students; and survey processing.

Data on behavior of students of the Faculty of Economics in Subotica, Serbia, on social media sites were collected through a questionnaire in June 2012. The questionnaire included 13 questions, with appropriate sub questions, given the total of 100 attributes. Questions were grouped into three sets that evaluate different aspects of social media sites usage:

- The first part of the questionnaire refers to the basic data about students from which can be obtained main demographic characteristics and previous success in school.
- The second part of questions is related to the familiarity of respondents with various social media sites, the frequency of visits to these sites, purpose and motives for networking and sharing the content through these sites, as well as the frequency of performing certain activities on these sites.
- The third set of questions examines the use of social media sites for a college selection, for the education needs (time spent online, frequency of content sharing related to the school, engagement in certain activities on these sites, and association with professors).

Additional questions were introduced. They refer to activities of respondents on blogs and forums, and the reasons for not using social media sites more frequently. A field is also left in which respondents could have written their opinion or describe their experience with the use of social media sites and networks.

The following of the paper briefly reviews the results of pilot study conducted in the third and fourth grade of high schools. The goal of pilot study was to improve the questionnaire by checking the clarity of formulated questions and clarification of potential ambiguities that may arise during completion of the questionnaire. Furthermore, to measure the time required to complete the questionnaire and to test the possibility of obtaining the desired results from the questionnaires. In the pilot study questionnaire was completed by 46 students, mostly by female respondents 67.4% (male 32.6%).

Each social media site has specific way in which user interact with the site itself and with other site members.

- Social bookmark – interaction is achieved through bookmarking the Web sites and search through websites bookmarked by other users (e.g. Blinklist).
- Social news – interaction is achieved by voting for and commenting on articles (e.g. Digg).
- Social networking – interaction is reflected in adding friends, commenting on the content of their profile, joining groups and discussions (e.g. Facebook)
- Social content sharing – interaction is reflected in the exchange of photos, videos and music, and commenting on other users' content (e.g. YouTube).
- Wiki – interaction is achieved by adding articles and editing existing ones (e.g. Wikipedia).

Due to the difference in the way of interaction on different social media sites, it is expected that different motives for using these sites and connecting through them are present among users.

Interaction on social networking sites is achieved through connections with other users and it comes down to the expansion of the network of friends, making comments on their content, joining specialized groups and discussions. The study showed that the most common social media site is Facebook, then Google+, and MySpace. Facebook is used on a daily basis by 78% of respondents, 4% do not visit, while the others use it every few days or weekly what's considered as frequent usage, Figure 1.1. The most frequent motives for using these sites are:

- maintain contact with friends – 97% of respondents,
- communication with other pupils regarding teaching materials, theses from school, help with homework and other educational purposes – 67% of respondents, Figure 1.2.
- 34% of active Facebook users use social media to monitor school activities (sporting events, school association, school organizations, etc.).

Particularly relevant for presented research are second and third findings which indicate that respondents, although mostly interested in entertainment aspects of social networking sites, also interact with the aim of improving communication, gaining information about class activities and obligations, as well as for successful resolution of school tasks. Thus, it is encouraging that a large percentage of respondents use these sites for communication regarding class activities, i.e. for educational purposes in general.

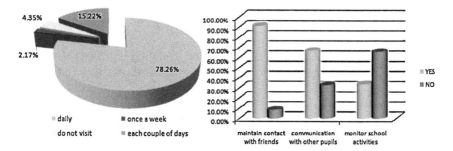

Fig. 1.1:   Facebook usage   Fig. 1.2:   Motives for Facebook usage

Social sharing, particularly pictures and video content, is the next aspect of social media interactions, where the interaction is reflected in the exchange and comments on the audio and video content from other users. YouTube, as the most popular site of this kind, is used by all respondents. Figure 1.3. illustrates frequency of use of YouTube.

Interaction on Wikis is achieved by creating and adding new articles and editing existing ones. All respondents know about Wikipedia, and it is frequently (daily, every few days or weekly) visited by 74% of respondents of which only 13% use it for educational purposes or school, Figure 1.3.

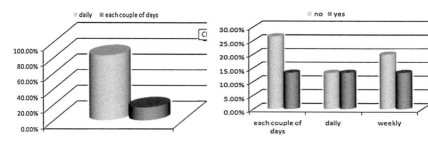

Fig. 1.3:   Frequency of YouTube usage   Fig. 1.4:   Wikipedia usage for educational purposes

The best-known microblog Twitter is not popular among respondents; 76% do not visit Twitter at all, even though all of them are familiar with it. Different way of interaction is present on Twitter, short comments, links, or any other content up to 140 characters can be posted.

Since blogs and forums are considered as most prominent data sources for sentiment analysis, finding that 7% of respondents are not familiar with the concept of blogs, and even 52% have never visited any blog can be considered as devastating. Only 24% frequently visit blogs of which 9% frequently write blogs and 7% post comments on other people's blogs. In addition, a large percentage of respondents do not visit forums, while it is frequently (daily, every few days, once a week) visited by 50% of respondents of which only 11% make comments, and 70% read the forum posts. For the purposes of education, only 10% of students use resources from the forum. This small number of people who often write blogs and post comments on forums is a group of influential users on the Internet that contribute to shaping public opinion – people who read these sources of information. Such findings posed the following question: as economics belongs to the field of humanities and social science, whether the activity on blogs and forums would be different if respondents are students from certain technical faculty. Also, whether their behavior on social media sites would differ much from the behavior of the students specializing in certain technical sciences.

Additional findings obtained through pilot study:

• The most common motives for social media sites usage, Figure 1.5, are: keeping in touch with friends, communication with other pupils about school, listening and watching online videos, sharing photos, music, videos, and other similar content, as well as search for quality content.

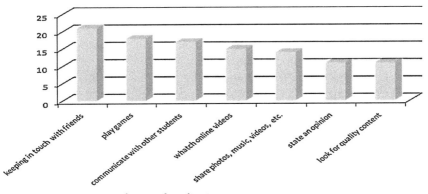

Fig. 1.5: Top motivation for social media sites usage

- Majority of respondents daily visits one or more well-known social networks, and watch and listen to videos, and at least once a week read blogs, forums or wikis.
- For gaining information about faculty and during faculty selection commonly visited sites were the official websites of the faculties, Infostud site (the most popular portal for employment in Serbia, which has a section devoted to diverse faculties), followed by Facebook and Google search engine through which they came to a different forums where current and former students of the Faculty exchanged experience. The largest number of respondents who have used Facebook in Faculty affiliation sought for currently known people that study respective Faculty.
- The respondents spent per week on average six and a half hours on activities related to high school. Frequent activities for this purpose are chatting, visiting social network sites, watch expert videos on YouTube, and read comments in the forums.

Although, generally speaking, the application of social media for education may not be frequent enough or qualitative enough, the majority of respondents, 72%, wish that social media is more involved in teaching process, which would certainly require greater involvement of both teachers and students.

Presented findings illustrate diversity in social media sites utilization among students. However, in order to develop true behavioral patterns of students, clustering data mining technique should be applied on collected data. As could have been supposed most frequently used social media sites are Facebook and Youtube. Given the fact that students do not connect over social media sites solely for entertainment purposes, but also in order to gain some additional knowledge regarding their education, to discus homework, connect in every possible way to improve their educational experience, therefore if higher educational institution wants to more comprehensively approach nowadays students it is of at most importance for them to engage in social media and to exploit these insights for conceiving the business strategy and for shaping marketing activities in accordance to students' behavior, i.e. as a reaction to their actions, as well as to implement Facebook and Youtube as a start in education or communication with students.

4. Further research

Knowledge gained through survey can facilitate definition of future analyzes that should be conducted on those data sources and definition of grouping criteria of attributes for such analysis. Firstly, clustering data mining technique should be applied on collected data in order to define groups of students according to their usage preferences and motives for social media connectivity.

Sentiment analysis is a complex analysis that takes time and requires many steps to be undertaken. The first step is to find and collect data – fetch, crawl and cleanse. The second involves text classification according to predefined keywords. The third step is entity extraction, followed by sentiment extraction, sentiment summary, and the final step is reporting and charting, (Deshpande and Sarkar, 2011). Certain survey questions should facilitate definition of search directions for qualitative text and content on the Internet for sentiment analysis, especially social media sites students frequently use, ways of social media sites usage – do students write blogs, leave comments, etc.

Through a short survey conducted over the websites of the major faculties of the Universities of Serbia, it was observed that a small number of faculties has its own official forum (36.5%), while an even smaller number of faculties has a blog (4.7%). Therefore, it can not be expected to find large amount of data available on forums and blogs that will be input for sentiment analysis, since most students do not have the habit of writing blogs and forums. In addition, the analysis showed that 33% of most prominent faculties have their official Facebook page where official announcements are placed. However, the exchange of views and communication of students is performed mainly in closed Facebook groups opened by the students. This fact indicates the existence of a problem in communication between the students and institutions and their habit to express themselves freely in a space that is not publicly available. Consequently this may compromise the relevance of the results of the content analysis of social media due to the unavailability of sources that probably reflect the truest reality.

Presented observations, as well as the whole research, are limited to students of the Faculty of Economics. In order to create the possibility of generalization of the conclusions it is necessary to conduct a comprehensive research and cover all the faculties of economics in Serbia for sentiment analysis, and perform a parallel analysis of the results obtained by individual faculties. In addition, coverage of all profiles of students at the University of Novi Sad (which Faculty of Economics Subotica belongs to) could identify different profiles of use of social media and recognize differences in habits and behavior on social media sites in accordance to different profiles of studies.

5. Conclusion

Process of sentiment analysis is time consuming, therefore the conducted research should have set the grounds for its realization on Faculty of Economics Subotica, with a particular focus on behavior of students on social media sites and potential data sources for the first phase of sentiment analysis. Research results showed that the most popular social media site is Facebook, that students do not engage in social media activities solely for entertainment purposes but they connect also for educational purposes. Even though small portion of surveyed pupils used social media sites for educational purposes, most of them wish for its extent usage in education. Also, given the fact that many students search the Internet through Google search engine and Facebook for additional information has set the grounds for believe that researched data sources could form their opinions about the Faculty and particular courses. As the survey results showed there is a solid ground for sentiment analysis application on these data sources. Potential analyzes that could be implemented are reflected in the use of clustering approaches to group positive, negative and neutral comments by courses, subjects, and the general sentiment and opinion about the faculty. It would also be necessary to monitor these indicators over time and to store the results in the data warehouse, and analyze whether over time there is a change in the number of positive and negative comments that would indicate respectively the improvement or deterioration in sentiment over time. These steps and analysis are the next phase of our research. An overall conclusion is that faculties should use social media analytics in order to get familiar with students preferences, habits and desires that would improve their relationships and enable faculties to build services tailored to modern students' profiles.

Bibliography

Casoto, P., Dattolo, A. and Tasso, C. 2008. *Sentiment Classification for the Italian Language: a Case Study on Movie Reviews*, Journal of Internet Technology, Special issue on Intelligent Agent and Knowledge Mining, 9(4): 365–373.

Deshpande, M. and Sarkar, A. 2011. *BI and Sentiment analysis*, Business intelligence journal 15(2): 41–51.

HP 2012. *Unlock the value of social media data*, http://www8.hp.com/h20195/v2/GetDoc ument.aspx?docname=4AA3–4229ENW, downloaded: January 10th 2012.

Junco, R. 2011. *The relationship between frequency of Facebook use, participation in Facebook activities, and student engagement*, Computer & Education Elsevier 58: 162–171.

Martin, C. 2012. *Social networking usage and grades among college students*, http://www.unh.edu/news/docs/UNHsocialmedia.pdf, downloaded: January 10th, 2012.

Ologie 2012. *Social media and higher education*, http://www.slideshare.net/leighhouse/social-media-higher-ed, downloaded: January 5th 2012.

Pang, B. and Lee, L. 2008. *Opinion Mining and Sentiment Analysis*, Now Publishers Inc.

Pearson Learning Solutions, 2010. *Pearson Social Media Survey*, http://www.slideshare.net/PearsonLearningSolutions/pearson-socialmediasurvey2010, downloaded: January 10th 2012.

Salvetti, F., Lewis, S. and Reichenbach, C. 2004. *Impact of lexical filtering on overall opinion polarity identification*, AAAI Spring Symposium on Exploring Attitude and Affect in Text: Theories and Applications, Standford University.

Study of Organized Cybercrime and Information Warfare

Igor Bernik, Kaja Prislan

Faculty of Criminal Justice and Security,
University of Maribor, Slovenia

Abstract

The current social conditions, which are reflected in the strained international relations, extremist beliefs, aggressive rivalry for the competitive and economic advantage and a high need for information power, have caused unpredictable changes in the threat posed by cybercrime. Due to the advantages of cyberspace, which allows for the anonymous, uncontrolled and unrestricted use, the realization of political, organizational and ideological malicious motives has become easier than ever. Modern information warfare, which is classified as organized cybercrime, is a security threat which causes dilemmas and challenges in terms of ensuring national security, economic stability and security of critical societal functions. This phenomenon has not been adequately understood or legally and formally defined from the security and political perspective, which makes it difficult to manage and sanction it. In terms of the perception of and response to this phenomenon, inadequate regulation puts victims in an unfavorable position. The author presents the results of research on the perception and the presence of organized cybercrime and concludes that such a threat poses a potential risk to the Slovenian business environment that is not adequately prepared to deal with current security trends.

Keywords

ICT, Cyber Space, Organized Cybercrime, Information Warfare, Organizations

1. Introduction

Relevant information has become the basis of achieving competitive advantages in all organizational structures. The power of information is most evident in international relationships, foreign policies, international economic competitiveness, and in the activities of ideological groups. Because information power has a crucial effect on success and because today information is mostly stored in digital form, attempts to establish information supremacy have logically migrated into cyberspace. This has simplified illegal use of confidential information and since enterprises have become a part of the global cyberspace and are now more dependent on modern technology, endangerment from cybercrime is also rapidly increasing.

Cybercrime is a relatively new form of criminality that has become widespread and a great problem because it compromises personal and organizational safety as well as national and international security. Cyber criminals have developed alongside information communication technology [ICT], and their activities are becoming more organized and sophisticated. The result is that the international political and expert public is now up against new aspects of cybercrime which don't just endanger individual users of ICT but put at considerable risk the stability of the global economy and international political relationships; the situation also affects the military preparedness of countries and the competitiveness of businesses.

The mobility of cybercrime and its ability to operate in different legal and cultural regimes are its main advantages, which pose, for now, a great obstacle for anyone trying to efficiently manage this danger. Sophisticated technology which has changed or lives has also created new dimensions of organized crime and thus new challenges for society. We are now in a situation where »organized« is combined with »cyber«. Offensive activities and the related organized criminality have always differed from classic criminality, especially in regard to how detrimental were the techniques used by perpetrators and how dire the consequences. This is why the migration of organized criminality into cybercrime is an even greater problem. Organized cybercrime is developing because of the growing need for »information power«. If the cybercrime techniques of achieving information superiority are used by organized groups, especially government agencies and corporations, than it's possible to say that information warfare is a threat from which no entity, that is a part of the global cyberspace, can be safe from.

The main problem facing law enforcement agencies is distinguishing between politically or corporate motivated and classic cybercrime, which can only be done, if the identity of the perpetrator and his motive are known. Determining motives can be extremely problematic, because anonymity and remote accessibility are the main attributes of modern ICT, enabling perpetrators to mask their identity and point of attack. The unmonitored global cyberspace, its anonymity and accessibility, legal constraints and limitations due to misconceptions of these problems are the main attributes of modern information warfare, which endangers every state in the world and each organization at the national level.

Information warfare can be defined as internationally organized and socially motivated cyber criminality which can have material consequences when a cyber attack is well planned, organized and coordinated. But it is necessary to point out, in discussions about the material consequences of such threats, that their reach is indirect. Even though we often describe ICT as weaponry it's really not a case of weapons of mass destruction but a case of having the means to massively disrupt information systems (Berkowitz, 2003). Because of the effect of information warfare techniques on society and life, these techniques should be labeled as a serious threat to international and national organizational and personal safety. States are those factors that should provide stable support to all other security levels. As was noted by Fritz (2012) a state can't provide adequate defense mechanisms against information attacks until it, too, masters information warfare techniques. This can be achieved by careful observation and researched of the said techniques.

Because of the wide and complex nature of information warfare, its impact on different social planes, and various techniques, our proposed definition is wider, but integral. The paper presents the findings derived from studies carried out in Slovenian organizations regarding their understanding of information warfare and its implications for organizational success and security.

2. Method

For the purpose of our research, we used descriptive methods and made a thorough overview of the literature, relevant research, and procedures that deal with modern information warfare.

We used the quantitative method of collecting data to carry out our study of information warfare in the Slovenian organizational environment. With the help of a questionnaire we researched 36 different Slovenian institutions, which are important from the information warfare aspect, and uncovered which threats represented the biggest danger to their databases and information security. The questionnaires were filled out by experts (75 % had college or university level degrees, 19.4 % had post-graduate degrees or a PhD), employees in information security and information technology divisions in different companies (in total more than 66 % of all respondents). 44.4 % of the organizations were from the public sector, and 55.6 % were from the private sector. Most organizations were middle size or big companies (in total 77.8 %). Data for the study was collected in November and December, 2011, by the »snowball method«. We observed the legislation and the ability of organizations to protect themselves from the threats. The statistical sample doesn't take into consideration the organizational diversification of the entire business sphere. The sample comprises companies of different sizes belonging to different industries, but all are relevant to cybercrime issues (we included educational, financial, and security institution, as well as businesses) and the abuse of information capital.

3. Researching the nature of information warfare

The advantages of power and efficiency lie with those that are the first to develop information warfare techniques. The information revolution, accompanied by globalization, the transnational economy, rapid exchange of information, easy access to the Internet and data of all sorts, have empowered individuals, corporations and states in new ways. The main goal of organized cyber criminals in the business and economic sphere is to gain an advantage over opponents by abusing confidential information.

Joyner and Lotrionte (2001) believe that information warfare techniques are activities used in times of crisis or conflict to achieve a set goal. More specifically we can define information warfare as protection, abuse, destruction or obstruction of information and information sources with the intent to achieve certain advantages or victory over an adversary (Taylor, Caeti, Loper, Fritsch and Liederbach, 2006). Information warfare basically means the acquisition and/or exploitation of information through ICT. Semantically, the term information warfare is a combination of the terms information and warfare. Information is a part of an information system; the system is the target of information warfare or tool used in information warfare, which comes as an information attack. Such an attack usually means breaking the law, policies and agreements, locally or globally, therefore, information warfare largely, but not exclusively, falls into the category of cybercrime. It should be noted that this is the modern understanding of information warfare, which was previously comprehended only in a military/political context. Based on what was written so far, we can define information warfare as:

>*Offensive and defensive activities of (private and public) institutions or groups undertaken to acquire and/or use information with the help of ICT to gain an advantage over competitors or adversaries. Simultaneously, the said institutions or groups try to protect their own information from misuse, damage or destruction. They try to block access to their information while trying to access the opponent's information.«*

Darnton (2006) believes that the main manifestations of information warfare are intentionally used to manipulate, destroy, and damage confidential information, which is most often achieved through malicious penetration, spying techniques, and remote attacks on information systems. Information warfare techniques carried out by a state are usually employed to collect information about economic, political, cultural, and military conditions in another state, or to launch offensive/defensive activities in cyberspace. In the first case, the state initiating information warfare is trying to achieve its goals by espionage; in the second case, the state's activities are similar to classic military operations, only that they are conducted in cyberspace.

Information warfare is not limited just to states, but is also used by organizations and businesses that need confidential data and information (to which they have no authorized access) to ensure their own survival, development, and competiveness. Commercial organizations dictate how society adapts to the information age and ICT. Those who successfully utilized the power of information and technology in competition with other subjects seize power and have control in the highly competitive business environment (Darnton, 2006). The main reason why cybercrime migrated to the private sphere (Slocum, 2012), is the possibility to establish a balance between unequal opponents; in fact it's a case of asymmetrical warfare where certain capabilities in the physical world don't affect the capabilities in cyberspace. The highest level of endangerment from information warfare is evident in organizational structures that are parts of the crucial infrastructure (Siroli, 2006; Europol, 2012) such as: information and communications, energy, banking and finance, physical distribution (transport sector) and the provision of vitally important goods to the people (water supplies, medical emergency services, government information systems, military information capital, etc.). Two sectors should be particularly emphasized when it comes to critical exposure, namely the electricity supply and information and communication technology that have an interdependent impact on other critical infrastructure (Čaleta and Rolih, 2011). Danger is present in all business areas, especially for successfully developing companies with information valuable to competing companies and countries (for example the automobile industry, pharmaceutical industry, and the computer and security industries).

Information warfare techniques, similarly as other forms of cybercrime, exploit vulnerability in security systems. Besides psychological operations and the physical destruction of infrastructure, information warfare techniques are the most commonly used by perpetrators when conducting cyber attacks. The basic tools of information warfare have been known for quite some time (Joyner and Lotrionte, 2001; Darnton, 2006; SANS Institute, 2013).

The most important techniques and methods are: using espionage software (sniffers, keyloggers, etc.) and sophisticated malware, DOS attacks, spoofing, information system break-ins, information theft, and social engineering. Besides these there are also other more common but less sophisticated ways to abuse information systems, e.g., viruses, worms, Trojan horses, spam, identity theft, blocking web pages, etc. (Svete and Kolak, 2012), but these usually aren't a part of information warfare because they're mostly in the domain of individuals with personal interests. The problem with information warfare is not linked just to the fact that it is difficult to comprehend and define, but also to its extent and implications. Illegal interventions by state organs, corporations and organized groups into computers or networks and communications represent an even greater threat to political and economic stability and security of critical infrastructure than classic criminality, because it also includes terrorist and military activities and advanced forms of stealing confidential information.

Computer technology has inevitably upgraded espionage, as it enables perpetrators to achieve their goals faster and with less effort. Anyone equipped with the right knowledge and technology can steal confidential personal or business data; this is nowadays done more easily than in the days of classic physical intelligence gathering. Besides, ICT is so pervasive and enmeshed with the business sphere that knowing how it functions is becoming universally vital. ICT is used in all areas of society and industries monitored by spies. A hacker breaking into an information system, contrary to a »classic« spy, doesn't need specific knowledge about the organization he is penetrating to acquire valuable data. The shift of information warfare activities and organized crime techniques into other spheres isn't just the consequence of increased competition and trends in capitalism but also a result of the current economic situation.

Security deficiencies exploited by information combatants largely depend on current social circumstances which effect organizational climate and structure. Downsizing the labour force as a consequence of a current financial and business crisis, has resulted in more out-sourcing, which additionally endangers the security of cyberspace and consequentially of information. The less there are employees responsible for information security the more vulnerable the businesses, especially because this situation leaves more space for mistakes.

Awareness of the importance of information and communication technology is on the rise in Slovenia, too. The trend is that state organs, government, and business entities are becoming more and more dependent on ICT, a situation, which automatically puts Slovenia among the combatants of information warfare. Even though the government might not realize it, its efforts to simplify critical functions have resulted in exposing us even more to adversaries. Consciously or not, the mesh of information systems and technology could have alerted information warfare perpetrators and drawn their attention to our information vulnerability.

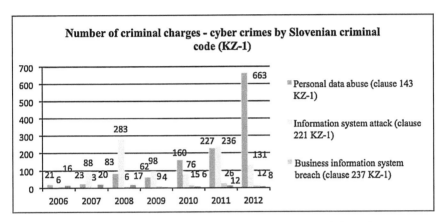

Fig. 1: Slovenian Police statsistic of cybercrime (source: Statistical data of crime, 2007–2013)

On the contrary previous studies (Bernik and Meško, 2011) have shown that the general public isn't well informed about or aware of cyber threats and the related legislation, therefore the conditions in Slovenia are not at all good. The current Slovenian information security strategy does cover the cyber aspects of security, but doesn't deal with these separately and thoroughly, and doesn't foresee the key element; cooperation between the public and private sectors to achieve adequate protection of the critical infrastructure (Čaleta and Rolih, 2011).

Police findings show (Figure1) that in the past years the number of incidences linked to cybercrime in Slovenia has increased in some areas (such as personal data abuse), but interpretation of official statistics must consider the underreporting trends in cybercrime and the fact of great threat from cyber criminality is also confirmed with the latest Slovenian CERT (SI-CERT) reports (Figure 2). They show that numbers of cybercrime incidents per year are steadily increasing.

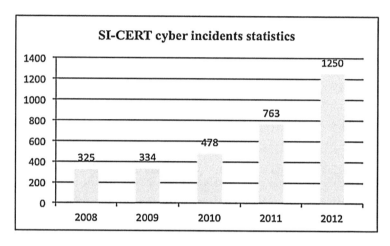

Fig. 2: Number of addressed incidents by Si-CERT per year (source: Adressed security incidents, 2009–2013)

4. Research Findings

The fact that Slovenia is also endangered by information warfare techniques was confirmed by the analysis of our comprehension of information warfare on our territory. Studies show that Slovenian organizations perceive information warfare techniques as threats to their information capital. All the organizations participating in our study without exception expressed worry and fear of such threats. Although we are lacking awareness programs on this topic our research has brought us to the conclusion that Slovenian organizations do understand what this threat means; more than 70 % of organizations included in the research believe that information warfare means techniques carried out with the intention of disabling an opponent's operations with the help of modern technology, which is a very accurate presumption. Organizations continued with an opinion that amongst different forms of powers, information power is the most important one for achieving superiority and outdistancing competitive organizations (50 %). By their belief military, political and economic power are subordinate forms of power, while information advantage is the most important factor of organizational success. Furthermore, organizations expressed the belief that the military, political establishment, and business sector are the main players in the information warfare arena, therefore, by their opinion, military techniques, propaganda, and industrial espionage should be the main forms of information warfare. The study identified the private sector as the area most threatened by information warfare – the most exposed being the computer, automobile, pharmaceutical and electronic industries, as they have the most valuable and desired data and information, and are active in research and innovation (Table 1).

Table 1: Information warfare as a threat to public and private sphere

Public sphere	Average value (3 point scale)	SD
Intelligence unit	2,67	0,63
Military organization	2,47	0,65
Public companies	2,28	0,70
Police	2,22	0,68
Jurisdictions	2,19	0,71
Legislative authority	1,89	0,71
Non-economic public services	1,86	0,72
Private sphere	Average value (3 point scale)	SD
Computer industry	2,69	0,53
Pharmaceutical industry	2,64	0,59
Electronic industry	2,47	0,65
Automobile industry	2,36	0,64
Media	2,25	0,65
Commercial industry	2,00	0,72
Ecology	1,75	0,65
Fashion industry	1,44	0,56

Regarding the identities of perpetrators of cybercrime the organizations pointed to their current and former employees as the ones most likely to endanger their information security and misuse confidential information (Table 1); employees were the greatest threat to the integrity of information (theft, abuse, or loss of data). This assumption is reasonable because employees have the most knowledge and the best opportunities to access confidential data. In addition to employees, hacker, spies, and competing organizations were perceived as the most likely subjects to partake in information warfare. Government agencies, opposing interest groups and ideological groups were seen as the least likely to break into information systems.

Table 2: Perpetrators of information warfare

Perpetrators	Average value	SD
Former employees	3.81	1.348
Current employees	3.69	1.142
Hackers, crackers	3.67	1.309
Spies	3.03	1.158
Vandals	2.97	1.207
Government services	2.22	1.149
Adversaries	1.94	0.826
Ideological/religion groups	1.58	0.732

The study confirms that the most common threats to information systems are also the most known cyber threats – spam, viruses, worms, Trojan horses, also slander and negligent employees. The least often encountered threats were espionage software, DOS attacks, and unauthorized access and control over information systems – these types of threats are considered the main information warfare techniques (Figure 3).

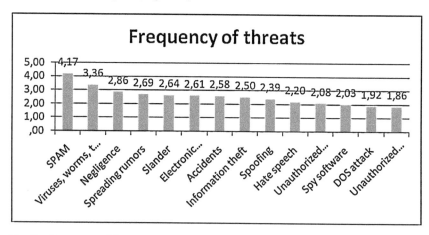

Fig. 3: Frequency of threats

But we also discovered that the most frequent threats are not the most dangerous ones. Organizations recognized unauthorized access to an information system, spying and spreading malicious software as the most dangerous threats, besides accidents and reckless employees. The most feared threats are also the main information warfare techniques. It can be deduced that of all cyber threats the ones listed represent the highest risk and danger to the success and security of organizations (Figure 4).

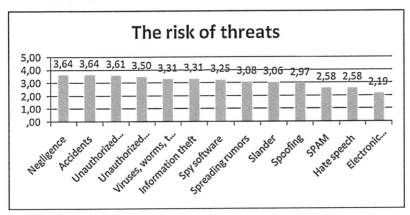

Fig. 4: The danger/risk caused by threats

After confirming the presence and danger of certain information warfare techniques in the Slovenian organizational environment we categorized, by using analytical group ranking, the organizations into two groups, based on the criteria how often they encounter threats to their information systems. We defined organizations in the first group as endangered, and organizations in the second group as secure. Contents analysis of endangered organizations showed that these are mostly large organizations from the public sector which are also active in foreign environments. This led us to the conclusion that endangerment of information systems is also influenced by other factors which should be taken into account when designing safety policies and implementing information security.

Contrary to our findings that information warfare techniques represent a serious threat to information security in corporations and other organizations because of their possibly damaging consequences, we found out that 41.7 % of the respondents believe that information warfare techniques could aid their organization's development and success. Furthermore 36.1 % of the organizations participating in our survey said that they accepted information warfare and have already used specific cybercrime techniques to achieve their goals. The most frequently used techniques were: spam (19.4 %), information theft and possession of confidential information (13.9 %), spreading rumours about the competition (11.1 %), and circulating viruses and other malicious code (8.3 %). A smaller percentage of organizations had used electronic harassment of clients and unauthorized access to an opponent's information system, but they haven't yet used more aggressive techniques, such as cyber terrorism, DOS attack or electronic espionage. Even though the majority rejects participating in such activities, these are nevertheless also used in Slovenian organizations and businesses. Slovenian organizations aren't just in danger of becoming victims of information warfare but also take on the role of perpetrators. 63.9 % of the organizations in our survey hadn't yet used information warfare techniques. If we consider the fact that many organizations do not want to admit that they have been engaged in controversial activities we can assume that information warfare amongst organizations is much more broadly used and that it represents an actual threat to Slovenian companies.

Slovenia isn't faced just with the problems of incomprehension of information security issues, but also (as are most other states) with related legal problems. The current Slovenian legislation thwarts detection and investigation of information warfare incidences. Slovenian enterprises don't have the means by which to legally uncover security incidences related to industrial espionage. The legislation covering cybercrime and the legal frame for its detection, investigation and sanctioning are the main pillars of an efficient security system protecting against malicious attacks initiated by information combatants. Without an appropriate normative basis law enforcement agencies can't wage war on cyber threats. The current legal solutions in Slovenia and abroad are proof that still not enough attention is given to information warfare. In Slovenia the legislators obviously don't comprehend the seriousness and severity of this danger. This creates circumstances in which it is far easier to perpetrate information attacks and steal data than investigate and prosecute such criminal activities.

5. Discussion

A quantitative and qualitative analysis of the state of information warfare internationally and in Slovenia confirmed the existence of techniques used by organized cybercrime in different spheres of society. Increasingly often these threats are realized in organizational environments, and in this respect Slovenia is no exception. The study confirmed the presence of different cybercrime techniques in various organizations, and the fact that information warfare is the greatest threat to information security. Now, more often than previously, employees (an organization's biggest capital) take part in such criminality. This means that the ones controlling an organization's assets – information – represent the biggest threat to it.

Research on information warfare perception among Slovenian organizations has shown that organized cybercrime endangers different business environments, the private sector is evidently more at risk, but the public sector proved to be more aggressive in using information warfare techniques. The complexity of cyber threats is evident from the fact that some forms are partially legitimate, which makes it hard to deal with the phenomenon, as we learned from the participants in our survey. In light of these facts, it becomes understandable why information security incidences are usually dealt with internally and rarely exposed publicly.

Regarding the aggressiveness and level of danger posed by different cyber threats, Slovenian organizations identified basic information warfare techniques as the most dangerous amongst all cyber threats, therefore we can conclude that organizations in Slovenia are aware of the gravity of the current situation in global cyberspace, but the level of their awareness isn't in proportion to their level of readiness and protection against such threats. This means that Slovenia and Slovenian organizations still have the need and also sufficient maneuvering space to improve strategies and operative guidelines to be able to oppose organized cybercrime.

The problems related to detecting and uncovering, investigating and proving incidences of information warfare are extremely vast and very much present. The current situation shows that the international community, as well as individual countries, doesn't give much attention to the specific threats of information warfare. This attitude is the consequence of incomprehension and a false sense of security. On the other hand, states – information combatants – which are currently setting trends in information warfare are well aware of the situation and know that bringing order to this area could cause them more harm than good. What, if anything, can countries and businesses do in these circumstances?

Unconventionality is the most pronounced characteristic of cyber criminality, and this fact should be considered when dealing with the phenomenon, therefore, innovativeness and unconventionality should also be used in our efforts to prosecute cybercrime and minimize its influence. Cyber criminals act outside all known behavioral patterns; they are quite unpredictable in creating and combining new ways to achieve what they want. These negative circumstances are compounded by ignorance and incomprehension at national and international levels, leading to the use of traditional investigative methods and procedures, which are not effective in cyberspace.

Firstly we should implement concise and comprehensive laws, and see to it that the public is educated about these matters. Law enforcement agencies should also act consistently, and especially know how to navigate around legal and cultural obstacles in tackling cybercrime which is global and international. The international community is obligated to provide conditions in which cybercrime can be appropriately addressed and prosecuted.

Corporations and other organizations operating with crucially important systems are responsible for upholding information security at the micro-level. This can be achieved by rising business ethics and by spreading security awareness among employees, users, business partners, clients and especially managements that have a direct influence on moral and ethical values within an organization. The right security classification of data and the limitation of the number of persons with access to sensitive data is a necessary step, which, together with the verification of all persons entering the physical space or cyberspace of an organization, helps mitigate risk and prevents many a danger. Most of all, it is necessary to implement consistent guidelines and standards at the national and organizational level to be able to: carry out efficient and detailed analyses of information systems; identify key vulnerabilities and exposed points; put in place the needed safety mechanisms. This is the only way to uphold the policy of uninterrupted operations as the primary goal of every state and organization.

To improve Slovenia's defenses against cyber threats, various organizations or all the different links in the Slovenian information infrastructure should cooperate amongst themselves. Even though the need for cooperation between public and private institutions in maintaining cyber security has already been identified at the international level, Slovenia still has not officially raised relevant questions. Because much of the Slovenian critical infrastructure is in private corporate ownership co-operation between the private and public sector would be a basic requirement in the effort to efficiently manage national information security.

In conclusion, information warfare poses dangers to all organizations with any sort of important information capital and which also participate in cyberspace. In future cyber threats will only become more pronounced and devastating, so it is necessary to focus attention on establishing cooperation between organizations from all economic sectors and also at the national level. It is important to correctly comprehend cyberspace as it is – a »place« where perpetrators and threats know no national borders or physical limitations. Organizations and governments should be equally »mobile«; international cooperation should transcend geographical, cultural, and legal obstacles, so as to keep up with the numerous perpetrators lurking in cyberspace. Governments and organizations should help the average or general user to become less vulnerable and to successfully avoid cyber threats at the work-place or at home. Ignorance is truly the weakest link in information security. It is not just groups of certain experts – information security managers and technicians – who need educational programs, but also all users of information and communication technology, and all who have access to classified information.

Bibliography

Alberts, D. S., Garstka, J. J. and Stein, F. P.: Network centric warfare: Developing and leveraging information superiority, Washington: DoD Command and Control research program, 2006.

Berkowitz, B.: The new face of war: How war will be fought in the 21st century, New York: Simon&Schuster, 2003.

Bernik, I. and Meško, G.: Internetna študija poznavanja kibernetskih groženj in strahu pred kibernetsko kriminaliteto [Internet Study of Knowledge about Cyber Threats and Fear of Cybercrime], Revija za kriminalistiko in kriminologijo, 62(3), 242–252, 2011.

Čaleta, D. and Rolih, G.: Cyber Security in the Operation of Critical Infrastructure – An Analysis of the Situation in the Field of Slovenian Defence, Contemporary Military Challenges, 14(2), 41–60, 2011.

Darnton, G.: Information warfare and the laws of war, in E. Halpin, P. Trevorrow, D. Webb in S. Wright (ur.), Cyberwar, Netwar and the Revolution in Military Affairs (pp. 139–153), New York: Palgrave Macmillan, 2006.

Europol: High tech crimes within the EU: Threat Assessment High Tech Crime Centre, http://www.europol.europa.eu/publications/Serious_Crime_Overviews/HTCThreatAssessment2007.pdf, downloaded December 23. 2012.

Fritz, J.: How China Will Use Cyber Warfare to Leapfrog in Military Competitiveness, Culture Mandala, 8(1), 28–80, http://www.international-relations.com/CM8-1/Cyberwar.pdf, downloaded November 10, 2012.

Joyner, C. C. and Lotrionte, C.: Information Warfare as International Coercion: Elements of Legal Framework, European Journal of International Law, 12(5), 825–865, 2001.

Obravnavani varnostni incidenti [Adressed security incidents], Ljubljana: SI-CERT, http://www.cert.si/obvestila.html, downloaded January 22. 2012, 2009–2013.

SANS Institute: Corporate Espionage 201, http://www.sans.org/reading_room/whitepapers/engineering/corporate-espionage-201_512, downloaded January 10. 2013.

Siroli, G. P.: Strategic information warfare: An introduction, in E. Halpin, P. Trevorrow, D. Webb in S. Wright (eds.), Cyberwar, netwar and the revolution in military affairs (pp. 32–48), New York: Palgrave Macmillan, 2006.

Slocum, M. Cyber warfare: Don't inflate it, don't underestimate it. O'Reilly Radar, http://radar.oreilly.com/2010/02/cyber-warfare-dont-inflate-it.html, downloaded December 20. 2012.

Statistični podatki za področje kriminalitete [Statistical data of crime], Policija, http://www.policija.si/index.php/statistika/kriminaliteta, downloaded January 25. 2013, 2007–2013.

Svete, U. and Kolak, A.: Cyberspace Security Relevance in the Time of Web 2.0, Contemporary Military Challenges, 14(2), 21–40, 2011.

Taylor, R.W., Caeti, T. J., Loper, K., Fritsch, E. J. and Liederbach, J. R.: Digital Crime and Digital Terrorism, Upper Saddle River: Prentice Hall, 2006.

Contribution

This paper was prepared with the support of the Lifelong Learning Program of the European Union, Project Competency Based e-portal of Security and Safety Engineering – eSEC, 502092-LLP-1- 2009–1-SK-ERASMUS-EMHE.

Secure Usage of Mobile Devices – Slovenian Survey

Blaž Markelj, Igor Bernik

Faculty of Criminal Justice and Security,
University of Maribor, Slovenia

Abstract

Providing security for sophisticated mobile devices is quite a difficult task. Even though numerous modern tools for ensuring advanced levels of security for users are available, these tools primarily deal with the technical aspects of supporting the safer usage of mobile devices. This said, the other factor in information security, the user, is often disregarded. Without constantly informing and educating users, data cannot be properly protected and information cannot be maintained. Numerous studies, including the presented one, show that users are not well aware of the dangers threatening mobile device users, and that they are even less informed about the, often freely available, solutions for protecting mobile devices and the access to data. In short, even the best technical solutions cannot help, if the user does not know which safety procedures to use. If would be sensible to outline guidelines for using mobile devices more safely, based on the data gained from the presented study and the data from studies conducted abroad. In accord with these guidelines, information security can only be established by interweaving advanced technical solutions with the unceasing education of users. In the future, the fast pace of the development of mobile technology will continue, therefore, it is imperative that the areas of information security are continuously upgraded, that new technical solutions are developed, and that each user of mobile information technology is well informed about the current trends in information security. It is important that users recognize modern mobile devices and are aware of the threats, that they can react to them, and, at the same time, have more trust in the available security solutions.

Keywords
Mobile Devices, Threads, Security, Slovenia

1. Introduction

Providing security for devices is primarily focused on technical aspects, but now, because of cyber criminality, this is no longer enough. Therefore, it's necessary to improve user awareness of security issues, so that they can fully make use of all the possibilities of modern mobile devices.

The purpose of technologically improved mobile devices is to better facilitate access to data which is vital for fast and efficient decision-making. It's therefore crucial that access to data is constantly available and unhindered (Hawick and James, 2002). The evolution of the Internet, mobile devices, cloud computing, and software, is to maintain a constantly available connection to corporate data, no matter where decision-makers are based and when they need to tap into relevant data. Results of a study conducted by comScore (2012) showed that in November 2011 the Internet was used by 380 million Europeans. Experts at Microsoft Tag (2012) estimate that by 2014 the number of mobile connections to the Internet will surpass the number of connections made by stationary personal computers; the current ratio is 50:50. The ability to be uninterruptedly connected to the Internet is what makes constant access to data possible, and mobile devices are the connective elements between users and data storages.

But constant access to data also has its downsides. Users of mobile devices can become easy targets of numerous threats (Kämppi, Rajamäki and Guinness, 2009) which can be realized by deploying malicious code, intercepting communications, mobile device thefts and others. Numerous global manufacturers and providers of security software report that there are more and more virus infections, cases of unauthorized GPS location tracking of mobile device users, misappropriations of personal and confidential data (certificates, passwords, etc.), and automatic incorporations of bits of malicious code. These are only a few examples of attacks which are now frequently being directed at mobile devices. These can also be labeled as cybercrime. Cyberspace provides numerous beneficial opportunities, but also dangers (Bernik and Prislan, 2012); and users' awareness of cybercrime is mostly influenced by media (Bernik and Meško, 2011).

Such attacks can be deterred only if users know certain procedures (and sometimes also the functions of hardware and software) and act accordingly to protect data from being alienated when attacks are detected. Corporations should educate their employees and inform them about security measures and the basics of protecting digital evidence, in case they experience threats or attacks, to increase the likelihood that perpetrators will be caught.

The information infrastructure within which data is stored should be designed to be compatible with the functions of mobile devices, but data should be sufficiently protected. In the past, the remote access was facilitated by an »open door« in the system's firewall through which communication could flow. Sophisticated mobile devices now constantly maintain connections with the Internet, and so communication mostly flows in a general way, as intended for web communications (browsing). This means that a door in the firewall is constantly left open and unprotected, thus increasing the possibility of a violation to the system.

In addition to their own information systems, more organizations are now storing and processing their data in a cloud. Because cloud technology works on an automated virtual plane the distribution of a system's resources is an automatic function of the system. It's necessary to provide sufficient protection from threats and see that digital evidence is properly collected in the event of a security incidence, so that the perpetrator can be detected and prosecuted. Detection is often difficult because a perpetrator's location is remote, and usually unknown. Users should also be careful when choosing their cloud provider. Increasing numbers of corporations are using cloud computing. This also means that the risk of experiencing threats is growing. TechNavio published a report on the current spread of cloud computing and the estimated future growth of these services – between 2010 and 2014 a 42 % growth rate is expected (Infiniti Research Limited, 2011).

1.1 Threats to Mobile Devices, to Data Accesses, and to Information

The weakest link in the whole process of storing and transferring data is the individual user, who is more or less educated about mobile devices, cloud computing, software, data transference, and the safe use of this technology. Increasing numbers of mobile devices were infected in the past few years. Both Lookout (2011) and Juniper (2011) regularly report more and more incidences of malware infections. The question is, why anyone would want to penetrate a corporate information system or cloud, since it's possible to get all data through mobile devices because these are so often used to access corporate systems via different networks. Because the number of mobile devices in use is steadily rising, threats are also proliferating. The IDC study (2011) showed that, globally, sales of mobile smartphones are going up by 50 % per year. According to the CEE Telco Industry Report, carried out by GfKGroup (2011) in 15 Central and Eastern European states, Slovenia is leading with the most smartphone users (27.8 % of Slovenians use smartphones). The second in line is Turkey (23.7 % use smartphones), followed by Lithuania (18.5 %). The more there are users of mobile technologies the greater is the exposedness of information systems to security risks. Threats are becoming more sophisticated and cybercrime is on the rise, because more mobile devices in use present more opportunities for perpetrators. As said, data which can be accessed by using mobile devices can be stored at different locations, that's why threats have to be categorized and each type tackled differently. Threats can act individually or in combinations (Markelj and Bernik, 2011), but always with the intent to alienate data. It is vital to identify: locations/points where threats could present themselves, the types of threats, and the possible misdeeds.

Corporate information systems and cloud computing can be especially vulnerable, even though indirectly, because of the use of mobile devices and (open) accesses to data, specifically when necessary security measures aren't used (e.g., authentication, encryption, tunnel protocols, secure Internet connections, etc.). Beckham (2011) drew attention to five major information security risks connected to cloud computing, compounded by mobile device usage. First there is the transfer of data between a corporate information system, a mobile device and cloud. Especially risky is transferring data by using various different Internet providers and simultaneously not encrypting data or using authentication and secure Internet connections (http, etc.). The second problem is the software interface, and the way in which users are verified when they access data in a cloud. Next come dilemmas regarding how data is stored, how it is diffused and encrypted. Is data encrypted all the time, even while it's being transferred to a device and/or stored on a server? The need to maintain a constantly available access to data and therefore being dependent on Internet connections is quite a big security risk.

1.2 Security solutions today

Mobile security threats come in many forms, and they are rapidly evolving. Many corporations now have mobility at the center of their IT strategy, and it will serve you well to put new emphasis on your mobile device security strategy (Mathias, 2011). Milligan (2007) noted in his article that corporations and other organization can't monitor something that can't be identified. What the author had in mind, were threats endangering corporations, which come with the usage of the rapidly evolving mobile devices and information technology in general. Therefore, corporations should constantly upgrade their information security policies and assess the risk of having their system breached. Corporations minimize risk by implementing hardware, which checks for potential dangers at the level of Internet traffic (Whitman and Mattord, 2008), and special equipment, which prevents invasions into information systems (Scarfone and Mell, 2011)). Some companies that are developing security software are already providing advanced software solutions for mobile devices (Schechtman, 2011), and firewalls, which monitor Internet traffic on the mobile device and the information system (Endait, 2011). Certain software enables corporations to define their own safety guidelines for the use of mobile devices (Mottishaw, 2011). Employees usually have passwords to wireless networks (Arbaugh, 2011).

Corporations can protect their data by using encryption software, but this method of protection is only as strong as the encryption key itself. It is possible to encrypt only certain segments of data stored on a mobile device, or data transferred through the Internet, or an information system as a whole. The encryption should in no way hinder the functions of a mobile device. Gilaberte (2004) wrote about various methods and algorithms, which can be used to encrypt certain data in certain ways. Corporations strive to achieve better information security, especially in regard to log-on procedures, and/ or the transfer of crucial data and information. This can be accomplished by implementing safer »http« data transfer protocols, and by authentication with certificates, as well as by encrypting and decrypting data (SSL), and also by the use of virtual private networks (VPN). Good examples of how the above-mentioned technology is used are bank portals and portals used for managing email. Certificates are used to authenticate the identity of a user when he or she tries to access these portals. Corporations try to protect their data by using strong passwords and authentication by a smart-card. Smart-cards can function only, if supported by sophisticated »background« technology. Most organizations set up virtual private networks to enable direct communication between mobile devices and their corporate information system or systems. This technology functions on the principle of establishing a »channel« between the virtual private network software of the mobile device and the virtual private network server located within a corporation's information system. Verification between a mobile device and an information system is done by using certificates – entrance to the system is granted once the identity of the user is verified (username, password). Zheng Yan and Peng Zhang (2006) noted that we should be aware of two crucial security weaknesses in the virtual private network technology. These are: (1) software for mobile devices and virtual private network clients are so diverse that it is impossible to guarantee that the technology will work flawlessly; (2) it is questionable, whether the software on a mobile device (including specific software used to establish a connection to a virtual private network) can be fully trusted.

Table 1: Solutions, currently used to maintain information security

Different Solutions For Maintaining Information Security Today		
Network	Mobile Devices	Users
VPN		
Encryption		Education
Authentication		Awareness
Firewall		Restriction
IPS, IDS systems		

Table 2: Solutions for maintaining information security which are no longer sufficient

Insufficient Solutions For Maintaining Information Security Today		
Network	Mobile Devices	Users
VPN (insufficient)		
Encryption (endpoint not encrypted)		Education (not for MD sec.)
Authentication (not always possible)		Awareness (lacking)
WAN integration (problems with insufficient integration within corporate WAN security)		
Firewall (insufficient)		Restriction (not present)
IPS, IDS systems (insufficient)		

Table 3: Quick overview of suggested measures for achieving better information security

Suggested Solutions For Maintaining Information Security		
Network	Mobile Devices	Users
Peer to peer not allowed	Authentication (password, access key, biometric access)	Awareness (report possible threats)
Searching for unauthorized usage network	Anti-malware and anti-virus software	Education
Accessing data just on servers in DMZ		
Remote wipe device		
Controls for traffic and applications using corporate network		
Policy for controlling and surveying		

As noted by Milligan (2007) some security measures in use today are inadequate protection for mobile devices against blended threats (shown in table 2). He also discloses which measures could significantly enhance information security in regard to the use of mobile devices. Some of the proposed measures are shown in table 3. The list of protective measures, as proposed by Milligan, is compiled on the basis of research, carried out by CIO Magazine and Price water house Coopers, of 250 organizations in Great Britain and other European countries, the USA, Canada and India.

2. Method

Understanding how smartphones are actually used is of crucial importance for technological development and the establishment of information security. It's undeniable that for students mobile devices have become an indispensable means of communication, so it's even more important that we find out with which elements of information security these users are familiar with, and use them, because this generation will soon be working in corporate environments and making use of different mobile devices. These issues were the basis for our online study conducted in December 2012. Our questionnaire was published on the web portal »1ka« (www.1ka.si) for 21 days. We alerted youth to our survey through e-mail, Facebook profiles, and in person. The questionnaire was designed so that we would discover how and why youth used their mobile devices; which devices and software solutions they preferred. The second part of the questionnaire was designed so that we could gauge users' knowledge and use of security measures, and awareness of threats that can endanger data security. The analysis of the compiled survey data was made with SSPS software tools.

Because some questionnaires weren't filled out completely, the sample population for some questions varies. Most of the respondents were aged between 21 and 25 years, in the next group were youth under 20 years of age. 61.5 % of the respondents were female, 63.2 % were male; all had secondary school level education. Table 5 shows what the respondents use their mobile devices for (in this case smartphones). More than a half of the respondents use smartphones for private purposes, while a quarter of them use them for private and work related purposes. Because of the chosen sample population, these finding were more or less expected (Table 4).

It gives us concern that the percentage of users who used the same mobile device for private affairs and business purposes is relatively high. This is evidenced by results regarding the question, which type of data users store on a mobile device? Table 6 shows which type of data the participants in our survey stored on their mobile telephones – most often a list of contacts, their names and GSM telephone numbers, photographs and video contents. This is all mostly personal data. Some of the respondents admitted to also storing some business data (names, addresses and telephone numbers of business contacts, e-mail addresses, important dates, certificates, etc.) on their mobile telephones. In case something happens (cyber threats) all this data is in danger.

Table 4: Characteristics of the sample population – users of the World Wide Web

		N	%
Age (n = 281)	Below 20 years	75	26.7
	21 to 25 years	133	47.3
	26 to 34 years	57	20.3
	35 to 44 years	2	4.6
	44 to 54 years	2	0.7
	Over 55 years	1	0.4
Gender (n = 275)	Female	169	61.5
	Male	106	38.5
Education (n = 280)	Secondary school	177	63.2
	1st Bologna level	67	23.9
	2nd Bologna level	25	8.9
	3rd Bologna level	11	3.9

Table 5: Smartphones are used for

Sample (n = 216)	N	%
Only for private needs	126	58.3
For private needs, occasionally also for business needs	56	25.9
For private and business needs	31	14.4
For business needs, occasionally also for private needs	1	0.5
Only for business needs	2	0.9

Table 6: Types of Data on Mobile Telephones

	YES (%)
GSM phone numbers	98.5
Photographs	94.1
Address book	67.8
Video contents	63.9
Important dates (birthdays, anniversaries, etc.)	60
Private e-mail addresses	40.5
Navigational data	30.7
Business e-mail addresses	25.4
Home address	21.5
Important business dates (business trips, meetings, etc.)	21.5
Business addresses	12.2
Certificates	2.4
Confidential business documents	1

The question is if their habits are already such that they have difficulty drawing a line between private and business affairs. How will youth use mobile technologies in the near future? Is it possible to change the present trend and ensure better security of data and information? It's problematic when private and corporate data is indiscriminately mixed without ensuring sufficient security. The results derived from a study conducted by Ponemon (2011) also showed a high percentage (40 %) of people who used mobile smartphones for private and business needs. We can conclude, based on the finding of Ponemon's and our own survey, that, in the future, it will be increasingly difficult to delineate between the private and business usage of continuously improving mobile devices.

3. Research: Security Aspects of Mobile Device

Data compiled in the course of our study showed us how the student population uses mobile devices and how they connect to the cyberspace. The goal of our study was to determine how well young users are aware of certain cyber threats (which can result in theft of data) and various protective measures which they could use to avoid security incidences. In our study the most commonly known threats are theft (89.4 %) and viruses (83.1 %) followed by bluetooth hacking, tracking, payment frauds, infections through applications, data alienation, interception of communications, automatic data transfer, browser infection, spyware infection, drive-by-downloads, malware infection, phishing, and rootkit infection. These findings aren't surprising, because these threats have been around for some time. It's quite a big concern that the youth aren't better informed about sophisticated malware which is steadily increasing in numbers. While bigger organizations regularly publish results of their monthly analyses, which show a steady rise in the number of mobile devices infected by malware, the results of our study showed that users aren't well aware of these threats.

Table 7: Protective measures for mobile smartphones in use

	I use it (%)	I'm familiar with, but I don't use (%)	I'm not familiar with (%)
PIN-code for SIM-card	89.6	9.9	0.5
Antivirus protection	29.5	49.3	21.3
Education	26.0	41.2	32.8
PIN-code for applications	21.4	56.8	21.8
Smartphone tracking	20.3	50.2	29.5
Archiving contents	19.5	44.4	36.1
Authentication	13.0	43.3	43.8
Remote content deletion	6.8	40.8	52.4
VPN connection	6.8	40.8	52.4
Central control	6.3	40.5	53.2
Data encryption	5.8	54.4	39.8

Table 7 shows some possible solutions which can protect mobile devices from cyber threats. Most respondents use standard PIN-code protection for their SIM-cards and antivirus software, but they aren't aware of more sophisticated tools, such as data encryption and remote deletion of data from mobile device. They do know about some other protective measures, e.g., PIN-codes, but they don't use them.

The question is why users don't use security solutions for mobile devices? Is it because users don't trust available solutions? This question was included in our questionnaire, for we hoped to illuminate this aspect of information security for mobile devices.

	Trust (%)
PIN code for SIM card	84.21
PIN code for access to mobile telephone applications	70.60
Antivirus protection	66.58
Enabled tracking of stolen devices	65.08
Tutorials	64.39
Data encryption	62.37
Authentication for specific functions	58.97
Data archiving	55.03
Central monitoring of smartphone (politicks of usage)	53.32
VPN connections	52.82
Remote deletion of mobile telephone contents	47.95

Table 8 shows the level of trust in specific security solutions. It was interesting to find that the level of trust in some solutions is relatively high. The highest on the scale of trust were PIN-codes for SIM-cards (84.21 %) and PIN-codes for accessing mobile telephone applications (70.6 %). The lowest on the scale was trust in the remote deletion of mobile telephone contents function (under 50 %), even though this possibility is widely available. If we draw correlations between the use of security solutions (Table 7) and user's trust in these solutions (Table 8), we can conclude that even though trust in some solutions is relatively high students don't used them.

It is a fact that young users aren't well aware of threats to information security and don't know enough about protective measures, therefore it's hard to prevent certain security incidences, misusages of mobile devices and data theft, even though some good technical solutions are available.

On one hand many corporations monthly publish the results of their surveys which all show steadily increasing numbers of smartphones infected with malware, on the other hand our study showed that the student population is ill informed and little aware of these threats. It's a fact that the youth of today will soon join the ranks of employees in corporations and other organizations where they will access and manipulate (corporate) data by using mobile devices.

4. Discussion

Mobile devices come with some protective measures preinstalled, but users often ignore these. Security depends on how much individuals know about the technology they use, therefore it's crucial to spread awareness and implement organizational policies to regulate the use of mobile devices, software, and accesses to corporate data in the central information system and/or cloud. It's necessary to evaluate which data can be stored on mobile devices, in the information system and cloud, and of course, if it's safe to access data from remote locations.

Figure 1 shows possible security measures that can be implemented on connections between mobile devices and central information systems and/or cloud – but knowledge and awareness are still crucially important. Figure 1 is based on theory and insights gained from our study. The conclusions drawn from the results of our study show a rising trend in the number of threats endangering users of mobile devices and all who access corporate data from remote locations. All mobile devices users should be informed which threats they could encounter, what the consequences could be, and be told how to avoid them.

There are available different methods of protection against cyber threats, but one has to use them. On the other hand, there are many ways to alienate data. The most common are: theft of mobile device, interception of data, and direct breach of an information system. Systems can also be breached by using decoding methods or by stealing passwords. But there are even more sophisticated ways which can »open a system's back door« or retrieve data by infecting the system with malware. E.g., infected mobile devices can automatically pass on confidential information to unauthorized strangers. This information can also contain certificates, passwords, and the location of the user.

Mark Fischetti (2011) made a list of the most common methods of alienating data. At the top of his list are violations of corporate computers and server systems (16 %). We can immediately draw parallels with the results gained through studies carried out by Lookout (2011) and Juniper (2011), which indicate a significant increase of different infections; and our study from 2011 of how one in Slovenia use mobile devices, how well aware they are of the threats and possible protective measures. Obviously, all three studies show the increase of malware, which means increased possibilities that systems will get penetrated more frequently.

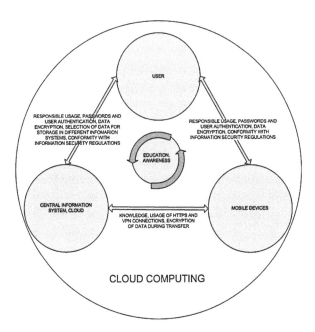

Fig. 1: Security measures implemented on connections between mobile devices and a central information system and cloud

The second most common method of data alienation is the direct »harvest« of data off the web. In this case also it's possible to compare the situation with an infection as perpetrators can access a user's data on the web only if they know his password to his profile or data storage in a cloud. It's interesting that in our study theft and viruses were at the bottom of the list of the data alienation methods most known by (young) users. Studies don't show a decrease in the proliferation of cyber threats to mobile devices, and consequently, a decrease in the number of misuses and data thefts – quite the contrary. Manufacturers of information security products are well aware of this fact. Industry guidelines imply further evolution of security software, especially of software, which will be activated (by a password) whenever a user logs-on to an information system, and will be in compliance with a company's security policy. Trends in information security solutions point towards bettering users' awareness of cyber threats, promoting knowledge about new technologies, and informing people about available protective measures.

Bibliography

Arbaugh, W.: Wireless Security Is Different, svn.assembla.com/svn/odinIDS/Egio/arti gos/.../Firewall/01220591_IMP.pdf, downloaded March 5. 2011.

Beckham, J.: The Top 5 Security Risks of Cloud Computing. Cisco blogs, http://blogs. cisco.com/smallbusiness/the-top-5-security-risks-of-cloud-computing, downloaded December 30. 2011.

Bernik, I. and Meško, G.: Internetna študija poznavanja kibernetskih groženj in strahu pred kibernetsko kriminaliteto [Internet Study of Knowledge about Cyber Threats and Fear of Cybercrime], Revija za kriminalistiko in kriminologijo, 62: (3) 242–252, 2011.

Bernik, I. and Prislan, K.: Kibernetska kriminaliteta, informacijsko bojevanje in kibernetski terorizem [Cybercrime, Information Warfare, Cyber Terrorism], Ljubljana: Faculty of Criminal Justice and Security, University of Maribor, 2012.

comScore: In Europe, Apple iOS Eco system Twice the Size of Android When Accounting for Mobile Phones, Tablet sand Other Connected Media Device, http://www.comscore. com/Press_Events/Press_Releases/2012/1/Nearly_50_Percent_of_Internet_Users_in_ Europe_Visit_Newspaper_Sites, downloaded February 2. 2012.

Endait, S.: Mobile Security – The Time is Now. Authorstream, http://www.authorstream. com/Presentation/snehaendait-477029-mobilesecurity, downloaded March 5. 2011.

Fischetti, M.: Stolen data: How thieves get your identity and other information. Scientific American, http://www.scientificamerican.com/article.cfm?id=data-breach-how-thieves-steal-your-identity-and-information, downloaded December 30. 2011.

GfKGroup: CEE Telco Industry Report 2011, http://www.gfk.com/group/press_informa tion/press_releases/008894/index.en.html, downloaded June 6. 2011.

Hawick, K. A. and James, H. A.: Middleware Issues for Mobile Business and Commerce, WSEAS Int. Conf. on E-Activities: Conference Proceedings, Stevens Point, Wisconsin: WSEAS, 2002.

IDC: IDC – Press Release, http://www.idc.com/getdoc.jsp?containerId=prUS22871611, downloaded September 9. 2011.

Infiniti Research Limited: Global Cloud System Management Software Market 2010–2014, http://www.marketresearch.com/Infiniti-Research-Limited-v2680/Global-Cloud-Sys tems-Management-Software-6458283/view-stat, downloaded September 7. 2011.

Juniper Networks: Malicious Mobile Threats Report 2010/2011, http://www.juniper.net/us/ en/dm/interop/go, downloaded September 10. 2011.

Kämppi, P., Rajamäki, J. and Guinness, R.: Information security in satellite tracking systems, 3rd Int. Conf. on Communications and information technology: Conference Proceedings (pp. 153–157), Stevens Point, Wisconsin: WSEAS, 2009.

Lacuesta Gilaberte, R.: Encryption tools for devices with limite dresources, 4th WSEAS Int. Conf. on Applied Informatics and Communications: Conference Proceedings (pp. 299–304), StevensPoint, Wisconsin: WSEAS, 2004.

Lookout: Lookout mobile threat report, https://www.mylookout.com/mobile-threat-report, downloaded September 10. 2011.

Markelj, B. and Bernik, I.: Kombinirane grožnje informacijski varnosti pri rabi mobilnih naprav. In Nove razmere in priložnosti v informatiki kot posledica družbenih spremememb

[Combined threats to the Information Security in the use of Mobile Devices. And new conditions and opportunities in IT as a result of social change], 18. Days Of Informatics in Slovenia 2011, Portoroz, April 2011.

Mathias, C.: Mobile Security Threats. TechTarget, http://searchmobilecomputing.techtar get.com/tip/Mobile-security-threats, downloaded October 20. 2011.

Mayer Milligan, P.: Business Risk and Security Assessement for Mobile Device, 8th WSEAS Int. Conf on Mathematics and Computers in Business and Economics: Conference Proceedings (pp. 189–193), Stevens Point, Wisconsin: WSEAS, 2007.

Microsoft Tag: Infographic Mobile Statistics, Stats&Facts 2011, http://www.digitalbuzz blog.com/2011-mobile-statistics-stats-facts-marketing-infographic/, downloaded February 2. 2012.

Mottishaw, P.: Policy Management Will Be Critical to Mobile Operators as Data Traffic Grows. Analysys Mason, http://www.analysysmason.com/About-Us/News/Newsletter/ Policy-management-has-become-an-urgent-issue-for-mobile-operators-as-a-result-of-the-rapid-growth-in-mobile-data-traffic-increasing-availability-of-flat-rate-data-plans-and-new-regulations-in-Europe, downloaded March 6. 2011.

Scarfone, K. and Mell, P.: Guide To Intrusion Detection and Prevention System. NIST, http://csrc.nist.gov/publications/nistpubs/800-94/SP800-94.pdf, downloaded March 4. 2011.

Schechtman, D.: IPad Security from En Pointe and McAfee's Mobile Security Practice. En pointe Technologies, http://www.enpointe.com/blog/ipad-security-en-pointe-and-mcafees-mobile-security-practice, downloaded March 5. 2011.

Whitman, M. E. and Mattord, H. J.: Management of Information and Security, 2nd edition, Boston: Course Technology Cengage Learning, 2008.

Yan, Z. and Zhang, P.: Enhancing Trust in Mobile Enterprise Networking. 5th WSEAS Int. Conf. On Applied ComputerScience: Conference Proceedings (pp. 1057–1064). Stevens Point, Wisconsin: WSEAS, 2006.

Process management: from early beginnings to complex simulations

Jernej Agrež, Nadja Damij

Faculty of information studies in Novo mesto, Slovenia

Abstract

Process management concepts have been present within the modern organizational development since its early days. Since then, we have been able to detect many changes, challenges and improvements that occurred in the field during the past century with the primary aim remaining unchanged: defining and optimizing organizational processes in order to achieve better business results. Comparing six different process modelling techniques, we choose TAD methodology for the basis of a process modelling and used iGrafx simulation environment for development of agent approximations process simulation. The significant contribution of the research is the presented approach, which is demonstrated within the context of the public safety and is further applied in regards to the missing person incident investigation. Missing person incident investigation can be described as complex process according to low availability and reliability of the information, together with unstable relations among entities that are involved in the process. With developed approach we analyzed such investigation and pointed out the critical success factors.

Keywords

Business process management, process modeling, process improvement, process simulation

1. Introduction

Taking in consideration commonly used set of approaches for organizational optimization, it cannot be neglected that foundations of process management have been recognized as important tool of modern organizations. Defining a process as a primary focus is enabling organizations to create a new base for establishing flexible, productive and innovative organizational environment. The process management chains together rise of organizational optimization and product quality value, but beside this also opens wide and at the same time precise perspective of observing, analyzing and manipulating organizational behavior.

Process management has been present in the field of public safety for a long time in form of standard procedures and regulations that define how field and administration work have to be carried out. Although public safety services base their actions on predefined processes, they face events that on daily base present risky and highly unstable environments where changes occur in unpredicted and uncontrolled manner. One of such examples is missing person incident (MPI) that present a very fragile part within the field of public safety, it is of great importance to be assessed and analyzed in virtual environment, but within a real life based scenario.

In the first part of the paper we present theoretical background of process management, together with conceptual evolution from early beginnings to predictions of future trends. We continue by selection, detailed description and comparison of process modeling approaches that allow translation of the model into the process based simulation, and thereafter use selected process modeling method for analyze of MPI and translation into the simulation, where we separated activity flow from decision making to be able to observe behavior of every single entity, influences and dependencies that they create.

Findings of the research propose analytical modeling and simulation solution that can be used for complex processes such as MPI cases. Due to single case that we used for setting up the modelling and simulation structure, we designed it in flexible manner to be able to insert new or discard existing entities together with calibrating their behavior patterns, according to data, collected from the new MPI cases.

2. Method

For purpose of first part of the research we used descriptive methods, overview of the literature, studied cases and relevant researches that directly included process management or held a connection with the concept. With the gathered information we constructed conceptual graphical model of process management evolution from the early beginnings until today. In following part we selected business process modeling techniques and compared them through the tabular comparison, to be able to select method for third, practical part of the research. In this part we firstly used observation method for collecting data that we needed to create a process diagram of studied case. With observation of process execution we were able to define process based behavior of 14 different institutions, organizations, informal groups and individuals that took direct role within the studied case. We carefully recorded 88 different activities within the process and entity based patterns that took the place during the process. Data for the study was gathered in May 2013 and thereafter processed with TAD methodology that was selected by previous comparing different business process management analytical approaches. For purpose of the process simulation and analyze we used iGrafx process simulation environment that allowed us to separate main activity flow from decision making, but at the same time make them interdependent.

3. Process management theoretical background

The process management chains together the organizational optimization and product quality value, "if one takes care of the process, the product will take care of itself; and any result is part of an endless process leading to future results and future processes" (Chung, 2009). Once we develop or apply a process model to a business system, it "help to produce more timely and accurate information leading to better decision making, help to improve transparency leading to better risk management, and help to improve auditing operations leading to lower compliance costs" (Cernaushas & Tartantino, 2009). Different process oriented approaches are set up on the same basic elements of business process recognition, description and modification that provides the framework for necessary adjustments or improvements within the organizational environment. "However, it is very dangerous to assume that simply copying either the business processes or the approach towards their improvement from one successful case to another will bring the same benefits" (Trkman, 2010). This is why, while defining optimization solutions, a variety of options are available: from applying the open sets with already defined and specific process oriented models measuring a development of innovative solutions for localized issues, which includes "gathering the information related to processes from different sources, monitoring these processes, and aligning them with corporate strategies and high-level goals" (Pourshahid et al., 2009).

To improve labor productivity Frederick Winslow Taylor was, in 19th century, first known to study different aspects of worker's characteristics. His management model was set on the practical specialization of work activities (Taylor, 1911). In this time parallel we cannot neglect Henry Fayol who advocated management is made of actions close to majority of organizations, which was confirmed trough the practical implementation (Brunson, 2008). At the same time Gantt designed tool later named Gantt chart that could be marked as a very first process model ever used (Gantt, 1913). Taylor's work was followed and upgraded by Henry Ford who developed a concept that was based on the principles of product standardization use of specialized equipment and reduction of workers' specialization for purpose of production (Tolliday & Zeitlin, 1987) and by Frank Bunker Gilbreth Sr. who introduced Therbligs – elemental work motions with aim to improve work results through the constant improvement of the working conditions (Nanda, 2006). According to George (1968) he was the first who introduced Flowchart and Functional Flow Block Diagram (FFBD) and also the first who implemented basic cyclic approach, indicated introduction in total quality management that was upgraded by Shewhart's work in 1945 and Juan in 1951 (Reeves1 1994). 1960s brought Petri net process modeling technique, which became popular in modeling and analyzing different kind of processes, from protocols to business processes (van der Aalst, 1998). In 1970s IDEF0 was developed, by US military for conducting analysis and estimations, and later evolved in its higher versions (Grover et al., 2000). Post-Fordism brought fundamental changes, comparing it to earlier Ford's philosophy: production line work got replaced by approach that supported learning, motivation and provision of know-how, to be able to guarantee the dynamic answers to the market demands (McDowell, 1991).

In early 1980s we can also find the first mention of a Theory of constrains brought new ideas about business planning that attracted many executives and production planners (Rand, 2000) as well as Total quality management (Powell, 1995). In this decade Toyota production system directed Toyota Company on a way towards one of the largest auto producers in the world (Fujimoto, 1999) and few years later Porter labels 1985 as a year of Value chain as a new presentation of organizations' activities. 1990s began with Rummler-Brache methodology, described in their book Improving performance (Rummler, 1995) together with Business process improvement (also known as business process redesign), described in James Harrington's Business Process Improvement: The Breakthrough Strategy for Total Quality, Productivity, and Competitiveness (Harrington 1991). This is also the period of Business process reengineering (also known as Business process innovation), which is defined as the global innovation and thorough change of business processes to achieve important improvements in performance measures such as cost, quality, service and speed of production (Hammer, 2013), enterprise resource planning was deployed and promoted among executives officers (Umble, 2003) and Lean production, Derived from TPS and influenced by Taylorism and Fordism, began its successful march (Womack et al., 201). Gupta (2009) spread importance of process based link with knowledge, today known as learning organization, together with Nonaka, who advocated understanding of knowledge within the frames of Knowledge management. Capability maturity model was developed that included set of criteria that can serve to improve organizational development processes (Paulk, 1993), Benchmarking was first time described as business tool in Boxwell's Benchmarking for Competitive advantage, and soon after, there was notable Six sigma breakthrough in General Electric (Eckes, 2001) together with Workflow management and its main purpose systematic process oriented approach (van der Aalst, 1998). In 21st century expanded Supply chain management, connecting organizations that ran operational and managerial value-adding processes (Lampert & Cooper, 2000). Capability maturity model evolved in Business process maturity model that is still subject of current researches (Hűffner, 2004), process architecture based management got introduced trough Service oriented architecture which revealed component based process view (Bieberstein, 2008), Process automation appeared together with Enterprise application integration. Both are symbiotically incorporated in process modeling (Linthicum, 2003), and Business process collaboration became very important part of modern global business development" (Gong et al., 2006). Business process mining appeared as useful tool for process identification and definition, with extracting knowledge about processes from their transactional log files (van der Aalst et al., 2002). In 2011 Business process model and notation 2.0 was released that replaced first generation of BPMN and became a standardized notation for the writing down the business processes (Allwayer, 2010). With the rapid development of IT technology, influences can be seen also at IS and its business part is not excluded. Real-time business intelligence is becoming decision driver, disabling process slowdown, and supporting transformation from short term Process management (Plenkiewicz, 2010) in Day to day process management (Cohen, 2010) and finally in Real-time process management (Smith & Fingar, 2002). It is not hard to indicate that from early scientific beginnings until today the development of following vertical structure can be distinguished: 1st is process modeling and 2nd is process improvement. Each of these contains many different approaches that use specific set of methods. From the horizontal point of view such structure is intertwined with similar western or eastern influences that are necessary for establishing connections and enable synergies among approaches and methodologies. Such synergies produce market products, suits that became known as Business process management systems that contain different solutions for specific demands and allow tailored accession to optimal results. BPMS can be identified as latest generation in the process management concept, because after a century of development, testing and spreading of process management structure, modern systems are trying to merge it together and use out the best of it: the perfect elements that will provide demanded solutions.

4. Process management conceptual evolution

At the early beginning of the research we discovered uncertainty among basic definitions concerning process management or business process management. Process management, based on a view of an organization as a system of inter-linked processes, involves concerted efforts to map, improve, and adhere to organizational processes (Benner & Tushman, 2001). We define business process management as follows: Supporting business processes using methods, techniques, and software to design, enact, control, and analyze operational processes involving humans, organizations, applications, documents and other sources of information (van der Aalst et al., 2003). Trying to understand the difference between two managing definitions we must define the difference between the processes that are their primal focus. A process is a completely closed, timely and logical sequence of activities which are required to work on a process-oriented business object. Such process oriented object can be, for example, an invoice, a purchase order or a specimen (Becker et al., 2003). A business process is simply how an organization does its work – the set of activities it pursues to accomplish a particular objective for a particular custo-mer, either internal or external (Davenport, 2005). The conceptual evolution map (Figure 1) enables us to get a clearer picture of the process management historical changes. The first half of our proposed time line presents approaches like: Taylorism, Fayolism, Fordism and Quality control that are representati-ves of constructed approaches, using several perspectives to achieve process development and optimization. On the other hand we can recognize approa-ches like: Gantt charts, Flowcharts, Functional flow block diagram, Petri net and Therbligs which are used for mostly for process description and explana-tion, without integrated tools to directly rise process optimization level. The following two decades defined on one hand strong approaches as Theory of constrains, Toyota production system and Total quality management that pro-vided the ability to change and improve addressed processes, while on the other new IDEF modeling approaches: IDEF0, IDEF1, IDEF1X and IDEF3.

Searching for connections among modeling approaches from 1900 until 1980, we can notice following similarities. 1st stage: Gantt chart acts as predecessor of Flowchart and Functional flow block diagram which can be also further evolved Flowchart with elements of Therblings (additional elements with new meanings). Fordism acted as an influence on later Taylorism. 2nd stage: Flowchart and Functional flow block diagram present clear foundation for development of Petri net and IDEF0 which use similar graphic notation for presentation of connections and activities. At the end of the period IDEF0 evolved in versions 1–3 that use very similar notation for information modeling, data modeling and process modeling. The improvement approaches in this stage present connection between Quality control and Total quality management. Less clear but notable is connection between quality twins and Toyota production system. Latter was originally called Just in time production and evolved in modern general Just in time philosophy that includes some elements of quality oriented approaches. Theory of constrains uses different, constrain elimination focused logic that highlights no obvious connection with the others in this period. Post-Fordism appeared as an answer to the market demands and implemented contra Fordism approach. There could be found some similarities with Taylorism. In period after 1980, during the 3rd stage: there was notable expansion of different approaches associated with improvement as well as modeling. IDEF pool got versions 4 (object-oriented design) and 5 (ontology description capture) and Benchmarking got introduced as a qualitative modeling approach. We can draw connection between Capability maturity model and Business process maturity which addresses CMM's process oriented features. There is also evolving connection between Petri nets and Workflow management. In this stage BPMN became standard in process modeling and in short time evolved from first to second generation. Service oriented architecture, complex and not primarily used for business process modeling can be, when graphically presented, compared with earlier approaches like Petri net or IDEF pool. Business process mining philosophy that stands on the time line in front of all modeling approaches derived out of data mining to enable process modeling in environment where other approaches fail to produce satisfactory results. Process improvement approaches within 3rd stage can be determined by following grounds, where evolution ties with previous stages get harder to distinguish because of numerous different interactions among developing approaches.

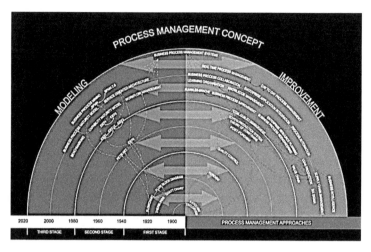

Fig. 1:   *Process management conceptual evolution map*

i.   knowledge (Learning organization in interaction with Knowledge management) influenced by Toyota production system;

ii. process core change (Business process improvement in interaction with Rummler-Brache, Business process reengineering) influenced by Post-Fordism;

iii. IT based (Enterprise resource planning, Enterprise application integration, Process automation, Business process collaboration) influenced by Toyota production system;

iv. interdisciplinary (Business intelligence, Supply chain management, Six sigma) influenced by Total quality management;

v.   quality (Value chain and its successor Lean production) influenced by Toyota production system, Total quality management and Post-Fordism;

vi. constraints (Day to day process management in interaction with Real time process management), influenced by Theory of constrains and Toyota production system.

5.   Process modeling for further simulation

Greasley finds process simulation as useful tool in change management within business systems (Greasley, 2003). Kano et al. argue it holds powerful analytical capability for evaluating business solutions (Kano et al., 2005), while Maruster and van Beest in their case study apply simulation dynamics to workflow models of activities and transactions among them (Maruster & van Beest, 2009). Approaches to business process simulation are set on comparable logics and used for similar purposes, but even though we cannot neglect discrepancies in details of individual modeling techniques, that serve as a starting platform for simulation development. Not every modeling technique is appropriate for simulation of any process dynamic, especially when our aim is to simulate process characteristics that were originally not meant as primary source of simulation.

For purpose of this research we will set our research problem scope to determine which of selected process modeling techniques shows the highest predispositions of being used for purpose of development and testing of external scenarios and integration in originally estimated business process simulation framework. We want to define usable, simple to understand and near intuitive simulation environment that will be "layer-based" (Chen et al., 2013) and "grid oriented" (Yin, 2010) and will allow us theoretical simulation, applicable on practical problems, concerning with integration of business process management and activity flow scenario analyses.

Process modeling with IDEF0 rules is a method, based on function which is defined as "a set of activities that takes certain inputs and by means of some mechanism, and subject to certain control, transforms the inputs into outputs" (Kim, 2007). It uses ICOM (Input, Control, Output, and Mechanism) concept as a main process presentation. "Function transforms inputs into outputs under the influence of a control, using the mechanisms provided. Inputs and outputs are information or physical objects. Controls activate or regulate or synchronize the function. Mechanisms are resources necessary to perform function. ICOM boxes are connected by arrows; outputs of one box can be inputs or controls of other boxes" (Kacprzak & Kaczmarczyk, 2006). IDEF0 modeling is simple and its notation is standard enough that it can be easily transformed in normalized database what practice results in many applications, developed on such (Hastings & Funk, 2008). But on the other hand time, such modeling approach causes inability to note time dimension, or to define correctness or conformity criteria in the model itself. Possibility exists to detect and highlight model incorrectness when it is originating in failure to follow the schematic modeling rules (Kacprzak & Kaczmarczyk, 2006).

We use IDEF3 for description of process flow. Plaila and Carrie described it as modeling method that enables possibility to discern what estimated system optimization is and what is prediction model of processes within the system (Plaila & Carrie, 1995). It presents "the behavioral aspects of an existing or proposed system" (IDEF, 2013). The most significant difference between IDEF0 and IDEF3 is that "IDEF3 does not let us create a model of the system, but captures precedence and causality relations between situation and events in a form that is natural to domain experts" (Plaila & Carrie, 1995). Models are presented by four types of elements that by description of Kim et. al are units of behavior (they define objects, time intervals in which they occur, relationships with other processes), junctions (logical mechanisms that define the time and relationship of single unit of behavior), links (they define destination of single unit of behavior) and referents (additional information about single unit of behavior) (Kim et al., 2001).

"TAD (tabular application development) is an object-oriented methodology. This methodology describes the functioning of the organization using several tables" (Damij, 2000). As Damij defines, the TAD approach results in tabular description and presentation of business process environment. It consists of entity table that defines and describes all subjects and their associations within the business system. Following table is named activity table and maps every single activity that operates as a part of the process and going even further, we design the task table that defines connection between entities and work tasks within every activity in the process (Damij, 2007). "Each activity occupies one row of the table. A non-empty square (i, j) shows a certain task or work represented by the activity defined in row i performed by an entity defined in column j. Developing the activity table is a result of interviews organized with the internal entities defined in the columns of the table. In the rows of the activity table we first register each activity identified during an interview and then link this activity with the entities in the columns, which cooperate in carrying it out. To make the activity table represent the real world, we link the activities horizontally and vertically. The purpose of defining horizontal and vertical connections is to define their similarity to the real world in which they occur" (Damij, 2000).

"The classical Petri net is a directed bipartite graph with two node types called places and transitions. The nodes are connected via directed arcs. Connections between two nodes of the same type are not allowed. Places are represented by circles and transitions by rectangles" (Han & Young, 2012). "When every place incident on a transition is marked, that transition is said to be enabled. An enabled transition may fire by putting one token into each of its output places" (Han & Young, 2012). Bobbio describes Petri net as a graphical visualization of activity flow within the complex system. Further, comparing the approach with the others similar modeling techniques, she finds Petri net appropriate way to describe "a natural way logical interactions among parts or activities in a system. Typical situations that can be modelled by PN are synchronization, sequentiality, concurrency and conflict" Bobbio (1990), and they have been "applied mostly in manufacturing and safety-critical systems" (Peleg et al., 2005).

"Gantt charts are widely used to represent production plans, schedules, and actual performance" (Jones, 1988). Pankaja defines Gantt chart as a graphical presentation of the work breakdown structure, combined with total time duration defined for single task, entities delegated to the tasks and overall process completion percentage (Pankaja, 2005). "Gantt gave two principles for his charts: one, measure activities by the amount of time needed to complete them; two, use the space on the chart to represent the amount of the activity that should have been done in that time" (Herman, 2010). Wilson further develops definition, explaining that Gantt chart logic in first plan uses systemic solutions and pays no attention to algorithmic solving of the problem (Wilson, 2003). "In a Gant chart, each task takes up one row. Dates run along the top in increments of days, weeks, or months, depending on the total length of the project. The expected time for each task is represented by a horizontal bar whose left end marks the beginning of the task and the right end marks the completion of task" (Pankaja, 2005).

BPMN is a modeling approach that consists of graphical presentation model, describing business process on the control-flow base with core graphical elements and extended specialized set. Recker defines core elements as a set that provides a graphical presentation for substantial business processes in simple, intuitive models, while together with extended specialized set, they enable presentation of advanced problems, such as "orchestration and choreography, workflow specification, event-based decision making and exception handling" (Recker et al., 2006). The approach is easy to understand and clear to interpret, but as Lerner et al. (2010) find out, not supported by formal semantic background, what causes risk that different process models are not understood equally, or on the other hand, designed almost identically but with discrepancy in their core meaning. Similar deficiency is described by Recker, who writes about lack of precisely defined and integrated common business rules, what causes additional need that user is forced to improve by himself (Recker et al., 2006).

Table 1:   Modeling approaches comparison

No.	Modeling approach	Type of mapping and notation	Syntax components (process components)
1.	IDEF0	semantically supported graphical diagram	box (function), arrow (input, control, output, mechanism, call)
2.	IDEF3	semantically supported graphical diagram	process schematics: box (unit of behavior), arrows (links); object schematics: circle (object), label (object state), arrows (links)
3.	Tabular application development	symbol based notation	entity (letter & numeric symbol), activity (letter & numeric symbol)
4.	Petri net	bipartite directed graph, symbol based notation	circle (place), bar (transition), arc from place to transition (transition input relation), arc from transition to place (transition output relation), black dot (number of tokens)
5.	Gantt chart	semantically supported tabular/ graphical diagram	timeline (time window), tabular columns (task, task hierarchy, task duration)
6.	Business process model and notation	syntax modeling, graphical diagram	circle (activity), box (activity), diamond (gateway), full arrow (sequence flow), dashed arrow (message flow), dashed line (association)

Table 2:   Modeling approaches comparison

No.	Primary dynamic	Secondary dynamic	Model hierarchy	Integration possibility
1.	function representing activity, process or transformation	fork (division), join (merger), node (parent box)	top-down decomposition	business process management, knowledge management, software engineering
2.	relations between situations and events	junctions (and, synchronous and, or, xor)	Situation/event based order	business process management, software engineering
3.	activity flow	decision (2 level division)	activity based order	business process management, knowledge management, software engineering

No.	Primary dynamic	Secondary dynamic	Model hierarchy	Integration possibility
4.	token flow	complex logical inter-actions	transition based order	business process manage-ment, knowledge manage-ment, information system engineering, reliability engineering, diagnosis, simu-lations
5.	accomplish-ment of a task in time	task order hierarchy	time and ac-complishment based order	project management
6.	events, activ-ity flow	looping, nest-ing, process break, transac-tions, sub processing,	activity based order	organizational modeling, function modeling, data flow modeling

6. TAD, practical application and process simulation

TAD represents simple concept for description of the organization using several tables (Damij, 2000). Originally intended for information systems development and business process reengineering it can be adopted for modelling a complex system. First and second phase of TAD methodology includes framework, how to capture and map system functionality that includes following tables: Entity table, Activity table and Task table. TAD methodology enables a creation of a model with any number of agent approximations (AA) that can incorporate any number of activities. We define AA as a decision making individual, pair or group of people that is modelled on a basis of real life events. Therefore such a model precisely summarizes process reality and maps it in digital environment. On the other hand, the reality based facts do not allow us to design true agents that would have the possibility of fully independent decision making. Their ac-tions are limited by activities and decisions that are part of modelled process.

The following real-life case is based on events that took place in May 2013. The entities involved in the MPI were the following: victim, victims' family, police patrol, police call center, individual police officer, Human rights ombuds-man, Prosecution service, public, SAR responders and Distress call center. Due to the privacy concerns no personal information that could reveal identity of people, who were involved in the case, will be revealed. The time scope of the incident was defined to be seven days according to most important activities that took place within the identified timeframe. Even though roots of the incident reaches far back in the past and consequences could be present long time in the future, we will not include them in the research scope due to indirect connection with the topic we present. MIP activities that remain in our research scope can be divided by days. Day 1: victim cleared internet history, temporary internet files, cookies and trash bin content with Ccleaner – software tool for PC optimization and cleaning. Day 2: victim left home between 8 AM and 3 PM. Victim had been seen in public the same day twice. First contact – 0,5 kilometer away from home and second contact around 4 PM and 1,8 kilometer away from home, heading approximately NNW direction. Day 3: victim had been identified on cash machine surveillance camera recording, approximately 40 kilometers away from home. New heading of victim's movement – NW. Day 4: victim's family asks for SAR responders to support the search. Day 5: victim had been seen 66 kilometers away from home. Heading remains the same – NW. Victim's family made contact with Human rights ombudsman and Prosecution service due to their dissatisfaction with police work. Around 10 PM family received an e-mail from the victim, explaining that the victim is alive and expressing few thoughts about dissatisfaction in life. Day 6: Victim had been found by family approximately 80 kilometers away from home in a shelter for homeless people. Day 7: Victim makes contact with SAR responders and eventually they meet, discuss the situation and decide how to close the case in constructive way.

We developed the model, beginning with identification of the entities that will take role as agent approximations. We adopted the entity table of TAD methodology and adjust it in form of matric system (Agrež & Damij, 2013), to be able to present how each AA influences another. At this point we defined the following AA roles: influencing AA (the one that triggers influence), influenced AA (the one that changes behavior under influence) and neutral AA (the one who influences only activity flow). Furthermore, we mapped MPI activity flow with the TAD Activity table, excluding any decision making. The activity flow consists of one beginning and one end, and in between all activities are lined up within the time order as it was in real situation. According to the fact that activity flow already took the place in the past, any additional decision making would present deviation from captured reality. From the present perspective, the activity flow is inevitable and should not be treated differently. Adjustments to the Activity table that we conducted are following: We added a column that defines the time dimension of the process and at the same time we implemented coloring of the patterns, due to weakly defined business process – work process relations of the MPI. Coloring of the patterns together with tabular separation reveals work processes within weakly defined environment more clearly and makes it easier to understand process intuitively. Furthermore we added the agent approximation matrix and model decision making agent approximations in additional layers of the activity table. Agent approximations were based on the decision making that follows the predefined protocols, law based directives, past experiences and knowledge, personal judgment, prejudice, emotional liability, or any other kind of influence. Not every agent approximation consists of all possible influences, but it is important to not neglect those that could importantly deviate their modelled behavior. We adjusted the activity table in a way that one agent approximation replaced several organizational departments and different kinds of influences replaced the entities. If we previously defined interaction in agent approximation matrix, we must now include AA as influence as well, but at the same time we must define such relation as activity in influencing AA, otherwise the influence is never realized but exists only as possibility. With the activity layer and AA layers we already got the general insight of influences in directions: influencing AA – influenced AA and influencing/influenced/neutral AA – activity flow. If decision making of single AA would be elemental, hierarchical and would not interfere within the itself, the number of possible AA influences would evolve in a predictable manner. Such a process would be simple to analyses but in fact it is far from real life public safety processes. According to high complexity of AA influences, it is necessary for us to develop a simulation that will incorporate and connect activity flow together with AA influences. For this purpose we translated the activity flow and AA tables into iGrafx process diagrams, Figure 2.

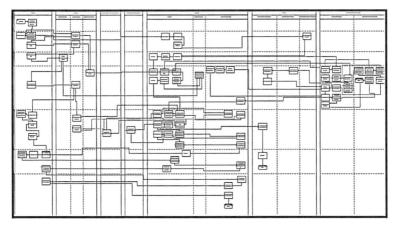

Fig. 2: MPI investigation process diagram

To be able to implement every AA into activity flow as an influence, we designed the whole MPI in single process layer, but created different starting points for each specific AA and for the activity flow. This is necessary for the AA to run with independent trigger that send activation signal (transaction). Furthermore we created the influence connection points, previously identified with TAD. For this purpose we used the attributes that are similar to the programming variables and can communicate data (information) and manage the flow of transactions through a process. For example, the attributes can set the duration of an activity based on the specifics of a transaction, control the flow of specific transactions through a decision output, or set global controls that can affect multiple transactions or activities (iGrafx, 2013). Through AA influences that are simulated as yes/no or true/false decisions and through the activity attributes we designed process scenario that reflected real MPI investigation. To be able to analyze it we ran the simulation with predefined analytical queries based on transaction count within the activity flow and decision making within every single AA that is supported by statistically based business process management approach Six sigma.

7. Discussion

Understanding levers of process management has been subjected to research from the beginning of 20th century by scientists, professionals and different organizations. With this paper we contribute to clearer identification of how process management concept developed through the century from time and interaction perspective. As a starting point of the research, we took the earliest mentioning of management as a part of science and then we divided the 20th and beginning of 21st century by three separations that mark periods of 40 years. In this time window, research indicates two general branches of process management concept evolution: modeling branch which sets its scope among identification, definition and mapping; and improvement branch that on the other hand reaches in a process itself with aim to raise its optimization level. Within these two branches we can witness appearance of different approaches among which some triggered further development of the whole branch or influenced long term concept evolution. In the modeling branch we can observe how approaches from first stage maintained their influence through the second stage until the third one when they hit the expansion of approaches.

The improvement branch shows us a notable foundation in first stage that lost its influence by the second half of second stage that indicates strong introduction in third stage where expansion occurs in the same time parallel with modeling branch. Even though we addressed both branches individually we cannot neglect their constant interaction which becomes even more apparent in the beginning of 21st century under the introduction of Business process management systems.

When selecting the most appropriate process modeling method that will allow further integration into the simulation environment, we took in consideration following criteria: 1) definition of organizational system framework, 2) translation in process based layers, 3) development and integration of scenario layers, 4) integration of additional event layers. Among six compared modeling techniques we selected TAD methodology that provided us with: the most precise definition of organizational system; simplest, tabular based multiple layer solution; highly flexible environment for modeling and integration any kind of scenarios and events. According to such range of abilities, we choose TAD as a predecessor for process simulation in iGrafx environment.

A development of the proposed process simulation solution and MPI case application provided us with the important answers concerning activity flow and decision making within the process. We were capable to determine the high importance of family's initiative to do whatever is necessary to find the missing person. As well we detect the crucial interaction among community, family and private support which present: wide range of information, momentum sustaining, special knowledge and information. Such interaction presents the critical element for the process to be realized within the desired output. The absence of any of these three elements would consequently lead to alternative ending that can only be predicted as what-if scenario and would not necessarily be realized. The simulation enabled us with another important insight to a MPI: partial endings of the process that are still treated as successful output even though the process itself never reaches the end as it had happened in real case. Such partial endings are highly correlated with family's priorities defining on how far the family wants to go into the investigation process. At the same time the results show us that if such partial ends exit, other entities involved in process could take partial end as the final end, and drop out of the activity flow, according to their regulations, practice, etc. Work of entities that are considered as public services presented 18% of all activities within the investigation. Remaining 82% of activities were conducted by two groups of entities; the major group with 64% of activities represents the people that were involved in investigation in completely private manner, and the 18% presents the entities that used their official public status to provide information and knowledge for private investigation. In fact they were acting against the law and could be prosecuted for abusing their position, even though they present one of the three critical success factors of the investigation.

In conclusion, process management evolved from observation and analysis of simple manufacturing actions into approach that enables us complete mapping of the complex organizational system within the virtual environments, where we get the possibility to modify existing process, observe triggered changes and their consequences. Solutions like this meet the trend of: real-time process capturing, monitoring and modification as a process management systems, by introducing such parallel environments that provide us with ability of critical comparison between launched simulation and ongoing real life process.

8. Acknowledgements

This research has been financed by the Slovenian Research Agency ARRS, Young researcher programme, ARRS-SP-2784/13.

Creative Core FISNM-3330–13-500033 'Simulations' project funded by the European Union, The European Regional Development Fund. The operation is carried out within the framework of the Operational Programme for Strengthening Regional Development Potentials for the period 2007–2013, Development Priority 1: Competitiveness and research excellence, Priority Guideline 1.1: Improving the competitive skills and research excellence.

Bibliography

Agrež, Jernej, Damij, Nadja: A layer-based, matric oriented business process simulation solution. Proceedings of the 7th European Computing Conference, WSEAS, Dubrovnik, pp. 167–172, 2013.

Allwayer, Thomas: Bpmn 2.0. Norderstedt, Germany: Books on demand, 2010.

Becker, Jörg, Kugeler, Martin, Rosseman, Michael: Process Management: A Guide for the Design of Business Processes. Berlin, Germany: Springer, 2003.

Benner, J. Mary, Tushman, L. Michael: Exploitation, exploration, and process management: the productivity dilemma revisited. The Academy of Management Review, 28(2), 238–256, 2001.

Bieberstein, Norbert, Laird, Robert, Jones, Keith, Mitra, Tilak: Executing SOA: A Practical Guide For The Service-Oriented Architect. Boston, MA: Addison-Wesley Professional, 2008.

Bobbio, Andrea: System modeling with petri nets. Downloaded April, 10th, 2013, from ftp://95.31.13.230/mirea/6/os-2010/petri/Petri%203D/Petri%203D/%D0%9A%D0%B D%D0%B8%D0%B3%D0%B0/miopetrinet.pdf.

Brunson, Holmblad, Karin: Some Effects of Fayolism. International Studies of Management & Organization, vol.: 38(1), 30–47, 2008.

Cernaushas, Deborah, Tartantino Anthony: Operational risk management with process control and business process modeling. The Journal of Operational Risk, 4(2), 3–17, 2009.

Chen, Peng, Zhang, Jiquan, Jiang, Xinyu, Liu, Xingpeng, Bao, Yulong., Sun, Yingyue: Scenario Simulation-Based Assessment of Trip Difficulty for Urban Residents under Rainstorm Waterlogging. International Journal of Environmental Research and Public Health, 9(1), 2058–2074, 2013.

Chung, H. Chen: It is the process: A philosophical foundation for quality management. Total quality management, 10(2),187–197, 2009.

Cohen, Oded: 24 – Managing Day to Day Operations. New York, NY: McGraw-Hill, 2010.

Damij, Talib: An object oriented methodology for information systems development and business process reengineering. Journal of Object – Oriented Programming, 13(4), 23–34, 2000.

Damij, Nadja: Business process modelling using diagrammatic and tabular techniques. Business Process Management Journal, 13(1), 70–90, 2007.

Davenport, H. Thomas: The Coming Commoditization of Processes. Harvard business review, 2005, http://hbr.org/2005/06/the-coming-commoditization-of-processes/ar/1, downloaded October 22nd, 2013.

Eckes, George: General Electric's Six Sigma Revolution: How General Electric and Others Turned Process Into Profits. Danvers, MA: John Wiley & Sons, 2001.

Fujimoto, Takahiro: The Evolution of a Manufacturing System at Toyota. New York, NY: Oxford University press, 1999.

Gantt, H. Laurence: Work, wages, and profits. New York, NY: Engineering Magazine Co, 1913.

George, S. Claude: The History of Management Thought. Newark, NJ: Prentice Hall, 1968.

Gong, Ruinan, Li, Qing, Ning, Ke, Chen, Yuliu, O'Sullivan, David: Business Process Collaboration Using Semantic Interoperability: Review and Framework. Semantic web – aswc 2006 proceedings, lecture notes in computer science; http://citeseerx.ist. psu.edu/viewdoc/download?doi=10.1.1.100.8485&rep=rep1&type=pdf, downloaded October 22nd, 2013.

Greasley, Andrew: Using business-process simulation within a business-process reengineering approach. Business Process Management Journal, 9(4), 408–420, 2003.

Grover, Varun, Kettinger, J. William: Process Think: Winning Perspectives for Business Change in the Information Age. Hershey, PA: Idea Group Inc, 2000.

Gupta, Aditya: Babur and Humayun: Modern Learning Organisation. Raleigh, NC: Lulu Press, Inc, 2009.

Han, Seungwok, Young Hee Yong: Petri net-based context modeling for context-aware systems. The Artificial Intelligence Review, 37(1), 43–67, 2012.

Hammer, Michael, Champy, James: Reengineering the corporation, a manifesto for business revolution. New York, NY: HarperCollins, 2009, https://www.google.si/url?sa=t&r ct=j&q=&esrc=s&source=web&cd=1&cad=rja&sqi=2&ved=0CC0QFjAA&url=http% 3A%2F%2Fcs5852.userapi.com%2Fu11728334%2Fdocs%2F8425ed172b16%2FReen gineering_The_Corporation_383831.pdf&ei=554PUam6BoffsgaX8oHADQ&usg=AF QjCNFgZDqAjPbSLaDZLUlqNFBGcY-kwg&bvm=bv.41867550,d.Yms, downloaded October 22nd, 2013.

Harrington, H. James: Business Process Improvement: The Breakthrough Strategy for Total Quality, Productivity, and Competitiveness. New York, NY: McGraw-Hill, 1991.

Hastings, R. Melissa, Funk, H. Kenneth: Improving the Navigation and Information Integration of Complex Process Models: A Case Study Using IDEF0. II. IIE Annual Conference. Proceedings, 1172–1177, 2008.

Herrman, W. Jeffrey: The Perspectives of Taylor, Gantt, and Johnson: How to Improve Production Scheduling. European Journal of Operational Research, 16(3), 243–254, 2010.

Hűffner, Tapio: The BPM productivity model – towards a framework for assessing the business process maturity of organisations, http://books.google.si/books?id=Bu XMmUiGNLcC&printsec=frontcover&dq=An+Overview+of+the+Business+Pr ocess+Maturity+Model&hl=sl&sa=X&ei=6zMEUcTbBc_ItAbzvoHoDg&redir_ esc=y#v=onepage&q=An%20Overview%20of%20the%20Business%20Process%20 Maturity%20Model&f=false, downloaded October 22nd, 2013.

IDEF3: Process Description Capture Method, http://www.idef.com/IDEF3.htm, downloaded October 22nd, 2013.

iGrafx LLC: iGrafx 2013 tutorials, http://igrafx.com/landing/download. html?name= iGrafx%202013%20Tutorials&ao_f=0137&ao_d=d-0001&c_type=c, downloaded October 22nd, 2013.

Jones, V. Cristopher: The Three-Dimensional Gantt Chart. Operations Research, 36(6), 891–902, 1988.

Kacprzak, Marek, Kaczmarczyk, Andrzej: Verification of integrated IDEF models. Journal of Intelligent Manufacturing, 17(1), 585–596, 2006.

Kano, Makoto, Koide, Akio, Te-Kai, Liu, Ramachadran, Bala.: Analysis and simulation of business solutions in a service-oriented architecture. IBM Systems Journal, 44(4), 669–690, 2005.

Kim, Cheol-Han, Yim, D-S.: Weston, H. Richard: An integrated use of IDEF0, IDEF3 and Petri net methods in support of business process modeling. Proceedings of the Institution of Mechanical Engineers, 215(4), 317–329, 2001.

Kim, Hee-Wong, Kim, Young-Gul.: Dynamic process modeling for BPR: A computerized simulation approach. Information and management, 32(1), 1–13, 2007.

Lampert, M. Douglas, Cooper, C. Martha: Issues in Supply Chain Management. Industrial Marketing Management, 29, 65–83, 2000.

Lerner, S. Barbara, Christov, Stefan, Osterweil, J. Leon, Bendraou, Reda, Kannengiesser, Udo, Wise, Alexander: Exception Handling Patterns for Process Modeling. Ieee transactions on software engineering, 36(2), 162–183, 2010.

Linthicum, S. David: Enterprise application integration. Boston, MA: Addison-Wesley, 2003.

Maruster, Laura, van Beest, R.T.P. Nick: Redesigning business processes: a methodology based on simulation and process mining techniques. Knowledge information systems, 21(1), 267–297, 2009.

McDowell, Linda: Life without Father and Ford: The New Gender Order of Post-Fordism. Transactions of the Institute of British Geographers, New Series, 16(4), 400–419, 1991.

Nanda, K. Jayanta: Management Thought. New Delhi, India: Sarup & Sons, http://books. google.si/books?id=VtjTyhi7g4QC&printsec=frontcover&dq=Management+Thought &hl=sl&sa=X&ei=y4UPUcGnHsGytAbfg4DgCA&redir_esc=y, downloaded October 22nd, 2013.

Pankaja, P. Kumar: Effective Use of Gantt Chart for Managing Large Scale Projects. Cost Engineering, 47(7), 14–21, 2005.

Plaila, Antonella, Carrie, Allan: Application and assessment of IDEF3 – Process flow description capture method. International Journal of Operations & Production Management, 63(1), 1995, http://140.118.1.131/teaching/BPE%20under%202005/IDEF3%20 paper1.pdf, downloaded October 22nd, 2013.

Peleg, Mor, Rubin, Daniel, Altman, B. Russ Using Petri Net Tools to Study Properties and Dynamics of Biological Systems. Journal of the American Medical Informatics Association, 12(2), 181–99, 2005.

Powell, C. Thomas: Total quality management as competitive advantage: a review and empirical study. Strategic management journal, 16(1), 15–37, 1995.

Rand, K. Graham: Critical chain: the theory of constraints applied to project management. International Journal of Project Management, 18(1), 173–177, 2000.

Recker, Jan, Indulska, Marta, Rosemann, Michael, Green, Peter: Business Process Modeling – A Comparative Analysis. Journal of the Association for Information Systems, 10(4), 333–363, 2006.

Reeves, C., A., Bednar, D., A.: Defining quality: alternatives and implications. Academy of Management Review, 18(1), 419–445, 1994.

Rummler, A. Geary, Brache, P. Alan: Improving Performance: How To Manage the White Space on the Organization Chart. Second Edition. San Francisco, CA: The Jossey-Bass Management Series, 1995.

Smith, Howard, Fingar, Peter: Business process management: The third wave. Tampa, FL: Meghan-Kiffer Press. Downloaded from http://uece-ees-t3-tcc.googlecode.com/svn/ trunk/refs/BPM-3Waves.pdf, downloaded October 22nd, 2013.

Taylor, W. Frederick: The Principles of Scientific Management, 1911, https://www.google. si/url?sa=t&rct=j&q=&esrc=s&source=web&cd=1&cad=rja&ved=0CCgQFjAA&ur l=http%3A%2F%2Fwww.enebooks.com%2Fdata%2FJK82mxJBHsrAsdHqQvsK% 2F2010-01-19%2F1263902254.pdf&ei=fYEPUZDmN8TMtAbK24DgBw&usg=AFQj CNE61fWfqnQgM-afIoCj1Aie1p6H4Q, downloaded October 22nd, 2013.

Tolliday, Steven, Zeitlin, Jonathan: Between Fordism and Flexibility, The automobile industry and its workers – Past, Present and future. New York: St. Martin's Press, http:// library.fes.de/afs/derivat_pdf/jportal_derivate_00020783/afs-1988-153.pdf, downloaded October 22nd, 2013.

Trkman, Peter: The critical success factors of business process management. International Journal of Information Management, 30(2), 125–134, 2010

Paulk, C. Mark, Curtis, Bill, Chrissis, B. Mary, Weber, Charlie: Capability maturity model for software, version 1.1., Technical Report CMU/SEI-93-TR-024 February 1993, https://www.google.si/url?sa=t&rct=j&q=&esrc=s&source=web&cd=1&cad=r ja&ved=0CCsQFjAA&url=http%3A%2F%2Fwww.sei.cmu.edu%2Flibrary%2Fabstr acts%2Freports%2F93tr024.cfm&ei=qqUPUfTNI4jNsgbQrIG4Bg&usg=AFQjCNH HJ-XIjMDguRIpIEX94A7vkbX8LA&bvm=bv.41867550,d.Yms, downloaded October 22nd, 2013.

Plenkiewicz, Peter: The executive guide to business process management: How to maximize "Lean" and "Six sigma" synergy and see your bottom line explode. Bloomington, IN: iUniverse, 2010.

Pourshahid, Alireza, Amyot, Daniel, Peyton, Liam, Ghanavati, Sepideh, Chen, Pengfei, Weiss, Michael, Forster, J. Alan: Business process management with the user requirements notation. Electronic Commerce Research, 9(4), 269–316, 2009.

Umble, J. Elisabeth, Haft, R. Ronald, Umble, M. Michael: Enterprise resource planning: Implementation procedures and critical success factors. European Journal of Operational Research, 146, 241–257, 2003.

van der Aalst, Wil: The Application of Petri Nets to Workflow Management. Journal of Circuits, Systems and Computers, 8(1), 21–66, 1998.

van der Aalst, M. P. Wil, Hofstede, H. M. Arthur, Weske, Mathias: Business Process Management: A Survey. Proceedings of the 1st International Conference on Business Process Management, vol.: 2678 of LNCS, 1–12, 2003.

van der Aalst, M. P. Wil, Dumas, Marlon, Hofstede, H. M. Arthur, Wohed, Petia: Pattern-Based Analysis of BPML (and WSCI). QUT Technical re-port,FIT-TR-2002–05, Brisbane: Queensland University of Technology, http://citeseerx.ist.psu.edu/viewdoc/downl oad?doi=10.1.1.11.7424&rep=rep1&type=pdf, downloaded October 22nd, 2013.

Wilson, M. James: Gantt charts: A centenary appreciation. European Journal of Operational Research, 149(1) 430–437, 2003.

Womack, P. James, Jones, T. Daniel: Lean Thinking: Banish Waste and Create Wealth in Your Corporation. New York, NY: Simon and Schuster, 2010.

Yin, Zhan'e, Xu, Shiyuan, Yin, Jie, Wang, Jiahong: Community-based scenario modelling and disaster risk assessment of urban rainstorm waterlogging. Journal of Geographical Sciences, 21(2), 274–284, 2010.

Fakulteta za
informacijske študije
Faculty of information studies

REPUBLIKA SLOVENIJA
**MINISTRSTVO ZA IZOBRAŽEVANJE,
ZNANOST IN ŠPORT**

Kreativno jedro:
Simulacije
Creative core: Simulations

Naložba v vašo prihodnost
OPERACIJO DELNO FINANCIRA EVROPSKA UNIJA
Evropski socialni sklad

»Operacijo delno financira Evropska unija, in sicer iz Evropskega sklada za
regionalni razvoj. Operacija se izvaja v okviru Operativnega program krepitve
regionalnih razvojnih potencialov za obdobje 2007-2013, 1. razvojne prioritete:
Konkurenčnost podjetij in raziskovalna odličnost, prednostne usmeritve 1.1:
Izboljšanje konkurenčnih sposobnosti podjetij in raziskovalna odličnost.